Adventures of a Bus Driver

by

Harry & Kay Jordan

The Pentland Press Ltd
Edinburgh Cambridge Durham

© Harry & Kay Jordan 1992

First published in 1992 by
The Pentland Press Ltd.
5 Hutton Close
South Church
Durham

ISBN 1 85821 008 9 597

Typeset in 10pt Times by
Print Origination (NW) Ltd., Formby, Liverpool
Printed and bound by Antony Rowe Ltd., Chippenham

To our son,
Jay,
and his wife,
Ellen-Ann,
with our love

Contents

INTRODUCTION

"Why don't you write a book about it?"

"About what?"

"The early days of bus driving." My wife's eyes glinted mischievously. "Then whenever you're tempted to tell me one of your yarns – for the umpteenth time – I can say, 'I know all about it, I've read the book.' "

I threw a cushion at her which she fielded neatly and put behind her.

"If *you* think my yarns are boring how can you expect anyone to be interested in a whole book?"

"It's only because I've heard them so many times. I've noticed when anyone hears them for the first time they think they're hilarious. Seriously, love, why don't you think about it. I'll help you."

I thought about it. I thought, "Why would anyone want to know about what happened over fifty years ago; who, in these days of fast cars, planes, satellites and nuclear power, would want to know about buses?"

Then I thought, "Why not? It's practically history. I remember buses with solid tyres; I remember being one of the first to have to take a driving test; I remember the days of bus piracy, when anyone with the price of a broken-down bus could set up in opposition to the bigger companies; I remember working seventeen hours a day for fourteen shillings a week; I remember – the things I remember would fill a book." So, I thought, "I'll try it. Whether I succeed or not remains to be seen."

CHAPTER I

EARLY DAYS

I was born in Featherstone, Yorkshire, a mining village, bounded by pitstacks, the local railway line and the main road between Pontefract and Wakefield. A grim, joyless place of identical terrace houses, two pubs, a Methodist chapel, a butcher's, a grocer's and, of course, a fish and chip shop. My father, Wesley, was a wagonwright at the local colliery and there were five of us, three boys, of which I was the eldest, and two girls. By the time I was thirteen I was in the top class at Gordon Street Elementary School and had no prospect of going any further. Secondary school education, whether at the Boys' Grammar School in Pontefract, or the Technical School in Castleford cost too much, and in any case, with seven mouths to feed we needed money desperately. I had to get a job. The question was, where? The obvious answer was the mine, but I was determined not to be a miner; so I had to prove to my parents that I could do something else.

Ever since I could remember I've had a passion for anything mechanical. A Meccano set handed down from a more well-to-do cousin was my prize possession and when, at the age of eight, I was given a steam engine I was in my element. All the models I built with the Meccano could now be set in motion and I spent many happy hours setting wheels and pulleys going until the day I ran out of methylated spirits, the fuel that primed my steam engine. It was a Sunday afternoon. The other kids had gone to Sunday School, but I had a cold, whether real or feigned I don't remember now. My mum was having a lie-down and father was reading the Sunday paper. What could I use instead of meths? In those days many people still used paraffin lamps

1

and though we had gas downstairs we still used lamps in the bedrooms. It struck me that paraffin would be just the job. I went into the coal shed with the engine and filled it with the paraffin and set it going. It worked like a charm, even better than the meths. Steam issued from the engine in steady puffs, wheels turned, siderods rotated. I was lost in my world of inventions.

"What's going on? 'Arry, wot are you doin'?" My father threw down his paper and I came down from the heights to find the whole kitchen engulfed in a black blizzard of soot. Paraffin wasn't as good as meths; unfortunately it wasn't smokeless. Rough justice was meted out for wrongdoing by my parents and I never saw my steam engine again.

But it would take more than a little setback like that to destroy my interest in mechanics and now at the mature age of twelve years and eleven months I had to find some way of working among engines, preferably car engines.

There was an opening with a local bus company for a conductor and while that could hardly be considered as working with engines at least it brought me in close proximity to them.

I got the job. I am sure the law regarding the legal age at which a young person could be employed was in effect at that time, but I was tall for my age and the man who hired me must have assumed I was fourteen. For the first two months I was learning the job which meant I got no pay, but I still had plenty of work to do and when I did get paid, fourteen shillings a week, I had to work even harder. I started at 6 a.m. and was supposed to finish at 11 p.m. We had no regular meal times only a ten minute break when we reached the bus terminal at Castleford and, when we were held up by mechanical problems or traffic jams, there was no break. Collecting fares wasn't my only job: I had to arrive first, fill up with petrol, check the water and drive the bus onto the stand. That was worth all the sweat, hunger and exhaustion – those few minutes when I had sole charge of the bus. I don't remember anyone ever teaching me to drive; I think I was born knowing, or else I absorbed it by some sort of osmosis.

At the end of the day I had to cash in, then sweep out the bus, clean the windows and leave all ready for the next day. I was rarely home before midnight.

Well it was a start, but my only chance of becoming a bus driver would be when one of the drivers left, but times were hard, jobs scarce and all the present drivers under thirty, so I looked like having a long wait. I'd been there about eighteen months when I heard that a smaller company was advertising for a mechanic and spare driver: a grandiose title for a dogsbody who would work all night servicing and cleaning buses, changing tyres and mending punctures and in return for all that graft would be allowed to drive miners to work from 4 a.m. to 6 a.m.

I'd learnt a lot about m.p.v.'s in those eighteen months by dint of hanging around mechanics, watching them work and asking pertinent questions, so I had no qualms about applying for the job, and because I was young and cheap I was hired for 16s. a week, hours 10 p.m. to 8 a.m., seven days a week and one night off a fortnight.

CHAPTER II

PASSENGERS

I'm not keeping this account in chronological order: how I changed from one job to another until I became a full-time driver, what happened when driver testing became compulsory, how unions came into the picture and finally how I coped with black-out driving during World War II. That's not very interesting even to me. I was more interested in people: the odd-ball passengers we had, the guys I worked with and the scrapes and difficulties I got into driving the broken-down machines which were all the company could afford. (This was long before the Rail & Road Traffic Act came into being.)

I'll start with passengers. They were, of course, our bread and butter – our *raison d'être* if you like, so we tried our best to look after them, keep on time, to wait if we saw an elderly person trying to run to catch the bus, not to stop and start too suddenly and throw the standing passengers off their feet, and mostly they co-operated – except for a few. Take Mrs Blackstone for instance. She was a stout black-haired woman with cheeks as hard and rosy as an apple. She was well dressed, always in black and she liked to impress people, even a common bus conductor. She got on the bus every Friday morning, a penny fare out of town and she always tendered a pound note. And there was Albert (my conductor) scratting through his cash bag to find 19s. 11d. Sometimes if we'd had a slow morning he hadn't enough change and had to let her ride without paying. That burned him and me; we knew well enough she could afford to pay.

Then one morning Albert got on the bus at the depot, grinning all over his face and patting his cash bag.

"Wait while Lady Muck gets on the bus 'Arry, I'm ready for 'er." He wouldn't say any more. We stopped to pick up Mrs Blackstone as usual and as usual she handed him a pound note. The driver's cab was open to the bus in those days and I could hear what was going on and see through the driving mirror. Albert put his hand in his cash bag and pulled out a blue paper bag – straight from the bank – containing £1 in pennies. He carefully extracted one penny and gave the lady 239 pennies, and pennies in those days weighed ten times what they do today. I had to concentrate on my driving after that and didn't see what happened, but I do know that, of course, she went to the manager and complained. Nothing happened to Albert though: everybody knew about Mrs B's 'winning ways' – so I expect he just got a warning. Anyway she always had a penny ready after that.

At the opposite end of the scale, it was a pouring wet day and Albert and I were standing under a shop canopy, chatting desultorily until it was time to start our next run to Leeds. A little girl came up to us. I'd have to call her a waif: her hair was hanging dripping wet, more like string than hair, her coat, miles too big for her, had the sleeves rolled up to free her hands, was without buttons and was fastened round her with string. She looked pale and woebegone and as if she hadn't eaten for a week, but she managed a timid smile.

"Please mister," she seemed to be addressing Albert, "does this bus go to Cutsyke?"

"Ay, luv, it does and you'd best get on it before you get any wetter."

She made as if to move, stared at us with unfocused eyes and then, graceful as a ballet dancer, she sank to the ground in a dead faint.

"Wot the 'eck!" Swiftly Albert bent down, picked her up in his arms and carried her onto the bus. I followed him.

"We'd best tek 'er to t' hospital." Fortunately there was a hospital on our route. Albert looked round for an empty seat. Just beside him a plump motherly woman was moving her laden shopping basket from the seat beside her.

"Put 'er down 'ere lad. I'll look after 'er."

He did so and at that moment the child opened her eyes. "I'm alright," she said faintly, "and I've got me fare." She held out a penny which she had clutched tightly all the time even when she fainted. "I didn't have no breakfast, but I'm going to me Auntie Dora's. She'll look after me."

The motherly woman nodded. "That's right, I know Dora Wainwright. You're Millie Davis aren't you?" Millie nodded.

"Me mom's been took bad, and me dad's at work – so I didn't know what else to do, but I've got me fare," she reiterated. "I took it out of me mom's purse."

"Ay, 'er mom's been took bad alright," said the woman dryly. "She often has." And she made a motion of lifting a bottle to her lips and winked knowingly at us. "She'll be alright now. I'll see to her." She dived into a brown paper bag and brought out an apple which she gave to Millie, who began to attack it greedily.

Relieved that all was taken care of, we both went back to work. I couldn't help comparing that little girl in her eagerness to pay her fare with Mrs Skinflint Blackstone.

One passenger I had great admiration for was blind, Mr Daniels. He travelled daily from Doncaster to Leeds and it was uncanny to see how he made his way among pedestrians on the pavement, how he avoided the posts that held up the shelters at Leeds bus station and crossed from one stand to another among oncoming buses. He always passed the time of day with us at Leeds: just "How are you? Nice day" etc. and seemed to know exactly where to address his remarks. It was many years later that I realized quite how acute his other senses were. I left bus driving for a couple of years to go into business and unfortunately I hurt my back through lifting heavy objects and had to go back to the buses. It was shortly after I came back when Mr Daniels approached my cab at Leeds bus station.

"They told me that Harry Jordan had quit," he said, "but if that isn't Harry Jordan driving I'll eat my cane."

"How on earth did you know?" I said.

"No problem," he said. "When you can't look out the window or read the paper, you spend a lot of time listening. I can pick out all the regulars: you all have your own way of changing gears, stopping and starting, taking corners and so on and I pass the time by listening and guessing who's driving. I'm nearly always right," he laughed. "We have to have some compensation for being blind you know."

There was another passenger who knew how to make himself objectionable and was very full of his own importance. He was the heir to a title and lived on a large estate about ten miles outside Doncaster and if you wonder why somebody like that would be riding on buses, he had a posh car and a chauffeur, but he also had a free pass on the buses (he was a friend of E.P. Bullock, the owner of the company) and he was a cheapskate.

Anybody would think he was the owner the way he liked to throw his weight about. The buses didn't run very often and they were nearly always full, with several people standing, usually more than the legal number – six – but you didn't like to leave people to wait another hour, especially when it was raining, but the Rt. Hon. Horace Smithers didn't care about that.

"You've no right to carry more than six standing," he said pompously. "It makes it very uncomfortable for the other passengers, besides being against the law. I shall report you to the Traffic Commissioners, young man, and I personally will see that you get the sack."

He said this to me when we stopped at Ponte, and I suppose he realized I couldn't do anything about it then (even if I would).

"So see it doesn't happen again, or you'll be for it and the South Yorkshire Motor Co." He strutted off twirling his umbrella.

"Are you going to do what he says, Harry?" asked Iris, my conductress.

"Maybe," I said non-committally, "and maybe not."

This was the time for fate to take a hand and a few weeks later she obliged. I'd been very careful in the meantime never to carry more than six passengers standing and touched my cap deferentially when Smithers got on the bus. Then one day it was raining buckets and the bus was full when we left Doncaster. We approached Smithers' bus-stop and I laughed aloud when I saw him standing there. Unfortunately there were two or three regulars waiting too, but this time they'd have to get wet. I slowed a bit as we neared the stop and the Rt. Hon. waved his arms and stepped out into the road yelling, "Stop! Stop!"

I swerved to avoid him, slowed a bit more and slid the window open.

"Awfully sorry, sir," I said in my best Mayfair accent, "I'm afraid we're full up. You wouldn't want me to break the law, would you?"

You can bet he lost no time in phoning Mr Bullock and he was in the yard waiting when we got to Ponte.

"Come into my office, Jordan," he said curtly.

"What's this I hear about you refusing to pick up Mr Smithers this morning?" he said as soon as we got inside.

As briefly as I could I told him what Smithers had said.

"Why that underhanded little bastard!" he exclaimed. "You did quite right to leave him and I hope he catches pneumonia. There's one thing certain, he gets no more free rides on my buses." He paused and seemed to be about to add something, then all he said was, "That's all, Harry."

I knew what he'd been going to say, "You don't have to stick to the law of only having six standing." But it was a by-law of the Road & Rail Transport Act and he couldn't come right out and say it was all right to break it. I sometimes think that if the folks who make these laws had to stand out in the rain for an hour or more they wouldn't worry too much if there were more than six standing. We tried to keep within the law, but sometimes you had to use your own judgement.

I could probably fill a book with stories of passengers, but it would get pretty monotonous, so I'll just end with a tale about a group of passengers who scared us half to death. It was fairly late at night at the Barnsley depot when a police sergeant came along with five guys in tow.

"Can I have a word, driver," he said. I got out of the cab and went over to him. "I don't like to do this to you, lad, but we've got to get this lot to Castleford. They're just out of Barnsley jail and we've no other means of getting them there except by bus."

In those days there were few, if any, police cars.

"I don't know if you've heard of them: the Hutchinson gang." I'd heard all right, who hadn't. The roughest, toughest gang of race course touts there were. They'd been in and out of jail countless times.

I looked at them. They were all alike with their prison-cropped heads, newly shaven chins and fairly clean clothes, and they all had that mean, evil look in their eyes, that 'don't-care-a-damn-for-you-chummie' look that made you very wary about crossing them.

"I don't think they'll be any trouble," went on the sergeant. "They'll know they'll be back behind bars in two shakes of a lamb's tail if they put a foot wrong. Don't you, Four-eyes?" he barked.

The only one wearing glasses grunted something.

"What's that?" snapped the cop.

"Yes, sir," said Four-eyes.

"He may not look it, but he's the ring leader," explained the sergeant, "and he's tricky – so watch out for him. I'll be off now. Good luck."

I thought to myself, "I'm going to need all the luck I can get." And after I swung the bus with the starting handle I was careful to take it into the cab with me. It was the only weapon I had.

There were only a few other passengers but one by one they left until there was only me and Ernie (my conductor). I was beginning to think things were going to be smooth sailing when one of them stuck his foot into the gangway and tripped Ernie sending him and his change bag flying. Pennies, halfpennies, tanners and bobs were all over the place and the crooks lost no time in scrambling for all they could find.

I didn't stop to think. If I had done I'd have been too scared to move. I rammed on the brakes as hard as I could and sent them staggering about like drunks. I grabbed the starting handle and barged into the fray. Deep down I was still scared, but I'm big and broad and with my weapon held up in the air I probably looked more frightening than frightened.

"All right," I snarled, "pick up that cash and put it back in the bag." "All of it!" I snapped as I saw one of them trying to put some change in his pocket.

I advanced on them threateningly, my faithful weapon still in the air.

It worked. They gathered all the money they could find and put it in the bag.

"Now then, sit down. You – there! You over here and you two at the back. And you," I pointed to Four-eyes, "you sit in the front seat where I can keep an eye on you and, if any one of 'em moves without me saying so, you," I jabbed him with the handle, "will get a crack over the head with this, so you'd better keep 'em quiet."

They crept to their seats like mice. I suspect that like all bullies they caved in when anybody stood up to them.

That was all well and good, but I wasn't sure how long they'd remain scared. Deep down I thought I'd be the one who'd stay scared.

We were only a couple of miles from the police station at Cudworth. I heaved a sigh of relief when I saw its blue light and began to slow down.

Four-eyes got up from his seat and began advancing on me. I stopped and grabbed the starting handle. What a change! Instead of threatening me, he was nearly blubbering.

"Don't hand us over, driver," he whined. "We'll behave. We won't put a foot wrong. Only don't get us sent back to jail. I couldn't stand it."

That wasn't surprising. In those days prison meant hard labour: bread and water and slops and savage reprisals for anybody who grumbled or caused trouble. I hesitated.

"Please." He almost went down on his knees. "I'll mek it worth your while." I drove on and we got to Castleford with no more problems.

There was a sergeant waiting for them.

"Everything O.K., driver?" he asked.

Four-eyes gave me an imploring look.

"Right as rain," I said.

"Come on then, you lot. Off home with you. God help their wives," he said to me and marched off.

As soon as he was out of hearing Four-eyes came up to me.

"Thanks, driver," he said. "I said I'd make it up to you." He handed me a slip of paper. "Put all you can afford on that, for the 2.30 on Sat'day."

Ernie and I were so relieved to have got rid of our unwelcome passengers we were like two kids let out of school: joking and giggling about nothing very much and it wasn't until the next day that I remembered the scrap of paper with a horse's name on it. I didn't have much faith in Four-eyes, but I did put half a crown (as much as I could afford) on and was delighted when I won over £3 – as much as a week's wages.

Don't get the idea that the Hutchinson gang had hearts of gold under their evil exterior. I just happened to have got them at a weak moment and I realized how lucky we'd been when a couple of years later two of them were hanged for murder at Armley Jail.

CHAPTER III

A LOAD OF TRIPE

Around this time, late twenties and early thirties, my regular conductor was a lad by the name of Albert Doughty. There wasn't much fazed Albert. He was a useful man in a scrap and in many other ways too as you will soon see.

I'm pretty tall, over 6'2", but Albert was taller, nigh on 6'5", and his height alone was very useful. If ever we had to come to a panic stop all Albert had to do was stand up straight and there he was, jammed between floor and ceiling, no chance of being shaken off his feet.

We didn't only carry passengers in those days: parcels, letters, milk cans and even livestock were crammed on the buses, the livestock on a carrier on the roof, of course, not among the passengers, and it was only small creatures like chickens and geese and rabbits. But the stuff we carried caused quite a bit of trouble from time to time. Take that basket of tripe, for instance.

The company had a contract to deliver this load of tripe to Barnsley market every Saturday. We picked it up at Cudworth, about six miles from Barnsley and it was collected at the bus depot in Barnsley. Well, one Saturday Albert and I were on the Castleford to Barnsley run and, as usual, we stopped outside the shop in Cudworth and the basket of tripe was loaded onto the platform at the back. It was a busy morning. Saturdays always were, but this morning was busier than usual. It was a fine summer day and everybody was off for a day's outing to Barnsley market.

Anyway we arrived at the depot not much later than usual and I went to the café for a cuppa, while Albert waited for them to fetch the tripe.

I got tea for both of us and drank mine and ate half my snap, but Albert didn't come. It wasn't like him to miss his tea, so I asked another driver to keep an eye on it while I went to look for him. He was standing by the bus looking this way and that.

"What's up, Albert?" I asked.

"They've not been for the tripe, 'Arry."

"That's funny. Stall should be open by now. Never mind, you go get your tea. I'll wait here."

We were due out again in ten minutes and Albert came back with about two minutes to spare and still they hadn't been.

Came time to leave, the tripe was still aboard.

"Tell you what," I said, "I'll drive round by the market. You keep your eyes skinned and see if there's anybody at the stall. You know where it is."

It was out of our way, but I wanted to get rid of the stuff. It was a big basket and took up a lot of room on the platform where the passengers got on and off and where the conductor had to stand when he wasn't taking fares; so we drove by, but the stall was deserted.

When we got back to Cudworth we stopped off at the tripe shop and Albert went in to report what had happened, and they said they'd call through to Barnsley and make sure there was somebody there on our next trip. Then we went on to Castleford. It's a roundabout trip, so the distance is nearly doubled and it was almost three hours later when we got back to Barnsley.

We couldn't believe it! There was still nobody there to pick up that damned tripe and, when we drove by the market, the stall was still empty.

Well, there was nothing else for it; we'd have to take the stuff back to the shop on our next trip to Cudworth. That gave us the worst shock of all. When we got there the shop was closed for the day! Now what to do? Very few businesses had phones in those days and we had no idea how to get in touch with the owner. We took that basket of tripe back to Ponte and left it at our company office "to be called for".

Don't think that's the end of the tripe story. There's more. When we finally got back to Ponte at 11:30 p.m. after a long, hot, tiring day we set off for the mess room to have a final cuppa while cashing up.

Albert was just going through the door when, wham! he was caught squarely across the face and chest with a blanket of wet, clinging, stinking tripe and then you couldn't hear yourself speak for the roars of laughter that followed.

It appears that nobody had called for the tripe and when the office closed the basket was dumped in the mess room. By this time, after travelling about the countryside for several hours on what was one of the hottest days of the summer, that tripe was making its presence felt in no uncertain terms. It stank worse than a pair of miner's pit socks at the end of a twelve hour shift. Some of the chaps coming off duty and discovering the source of the smell decided to put the tripe to good use and were enjoying a few laughs at their co-workers' expense.

It wasn't long before Albert and I got into the act and soon Albert had them all in stitches, as he cavorted about with a sheet of the stuff, pretending to be a ballet dancer, and every now and then stopping to take a swipe at an unwary newcomer.

At some point in the proceedings there was a lull. I think everyone had laughed himself breathless and was waiting for a second wind. Albert stood poised by the door, holding the tripe like a bullfighter with his cape awaiting the charge of the bull. Footsteps were heard, the door was flung open and he swung the tripe full into the face of – the traffic manager.

You could have heard a pin drop. If it had been the king himself who had been so assaulted there couldn't have been a more awe-stricken group. In those days when jobs were as scarce as hens' teeth you just didn't fool around with bosses, especially this one. He was about half the size of Albert, which meant that his face was just about level with the tripe held at the end of those chimpanzee-like arms, so he got the full impact of that offensive (in more ways than one) weapon. He didn't speak for about ten seconds then he just said, "Come to my office, Doughty." And turned on his heel and walked away.

Nobody had much doubt about poor old Albert's fate. He would be out on his ear, accident or no. Mr D. had a great sense of his own importance and an undignified assault like that was enough to infuriate him beyond all reason. The fact that it was the staff mess room and out of bounds to management wouldn't be allowed to sway his decision.

The other chaps went home soon after that, but I couldn't leave Albert in the lurch. He came in shortly after that, trying to grin and make a joke of it.

"He's had my 'ide, now 'e wants to see you, 'Arry."

"Good." I got to my feet. "Don't go away, Albert; I won't be long."

I went along the corridor to his office, tapped on the door and walked in. He hated that. You were supposed to wait till you were told to come in. I sat down without being told, another breach of etiquette.

"Sit down, Jordan," he said sarcastically.

"I'm sitting down, what's up?"

"Why wasn't that tripe delivered to its proper destination?"

"Didn't Albert tell you?"

"He told me some rigmarole about there being nobody there to pick it up."

"Are you saying he's a liar?"

"No, I'm just saying it seems rather fishy."

"Yes it was, bloody fishy, but it wasn't Albert's fault. And if you don't believe him or me you'd better get in touch with your friends at Cudworth and ask them what happened. Then p'raps you'll apologize to both of us."

If you're wondering how it was that I was so brave when everyone else was afraid of being sacked, I'll explain. There were two reasons: one, I was a strong union man and in those days unions were just beginning to get a bit of muscle and bosses to realize it didn't always do to antagonize them.

I don't want you to think that I still believe that unions are the answer to all labour disputes, but at that time they were the only weapon the working man had against some pretty despicable bosses. The other reason, and perhaps the more important one, at least in the manager's eyes, was that I and three other drivers were the only ones who could handle the broken-down machines disguised as buses that the company owned and they needed us more than we needed them.

Mr D. controlled himself with an effort.

"All right, Jordan, granting that his story is true, it doesn't excuse his behaviour in the mess room, clowning about like a school kid and hitting me in the face with the stuff."

"If you hadn't been snooping around where you don't belong it wouldn't have happened."

This time I'd gone a bit too far.

"I don't have to answer to you for my actions. Doughty is fired and that's the end of it."

"Oh, in that case I guess I'm fired too, and Baker and Huddlestone." – they were two of the drivers I mentioned – "We were all doing it." I got up to go. "I'll let them know not to come in tomorrow."

I got as far as the door before he stopped me.

"Oh, forget about it," he snapped. "Just see it doesn't happen again."

"Yes, sir, good night, sir." I closed the door quietly and went to let Albert know he was off the hook.

Another time when Albert and I got oursevles in a pickle was when we would have been in real trouble if anybody in authority had caught us.

We often had to pick up milk cans from neighbouring farms and deliver them to the bottling plant in town. They were big cans, holding about 18-20 gallons and they, too, had to be carried on the platform and were a bit of a nuisance. If they weren't well jammed into place they would slide about and get in everybody's way. On one occasion when a driver was taking a corner faster than he should have been, the cans slid right off the bus and landed in a ditch. It was pitch dark, and they had the devil of a time finding them.

But that wasn't on our bus. Our crime was deliberate and a lot worse than that.

It was a really hot morning although it was early. The farmers had to have the milk at the plant as soon after milking as possible. There was no one else in the bus and, as we were before time, I stopped the bus in a shady spot and went around to have a bit of a natter with Albert.

"Going to be a scorcher," Albert remarked as he took off his hat and mopped his forehead.

"Ay," I agreed, "hope it's like this next week."

Albert and I started our summer holidays then.

"You don't happen to have anything to drink, 'Arry? My mouth's like a lime kiln."

"I don't, but I could do with summat. It's a long time before we get a break. Wait on though, how about a sup of milk?"

"One thing I like about you, 'Arry, you never stick fast. There's just one little problem, though, what do we drink out of?"

That was a good question, and it wasn't one that was easily answered. A careful search of the bus, including the tool box, turned up nothing but an empty oil can. It looked as if we would have to stay thirsty. We took a last look around the inside of the bus and there, right at Albert's eye level was the answer to the problem: one of the glass globes covering the lights. With a wink at me Albert unscrewed the globe and there was the perfect drinking cup. Albert wiped it carefully with the cleanest duster he could find, dipped it into the milk can and, with a bow that would have done credit to Sir Walter Raleigh, he handed it to me.

That was the best drink I have ever tasted: rich, creamy and fresh from the cow. It beats all your ice-cold, pasteurized milk you get today.

Oh, I know it was probably laden with germs, but we didn't think about things like that in those days. Germs were for hospitals; fresh air, fresh food and exercise were what kept you fit and I sometimes think that the more you worry about getting sick the more likely you are to succumb to those sneaky little things. But I digress.

It was now Albert's turn and, seeing the look of ecstasy on my face, he just couldn't wait. He grabbed the cup, dipped it in the can – and dropped it!

We've laughed about that incident many a time since, but at the time it was not a laughing matter. If anybody found out we'd lose our jobs for sure.

But what could we do? Those cans were over three feet high. How on earth were we going to get the globe out?

"Only one thing for it, 'Arry."

Albert slipped off his braces, took off his shirt and plunged his arms into the milk, right up to his shoulder. A second or two's groping and up came the vessel – fortunately, free of all cracks or chips. There might be a few more germs in the milk, but at least there was no broken glass.

We held our breath for the next few days, but nobody said a dicky-bird. If anybody at the plant noticed that one can wasn't quite full, they evidently didn't think it was worth mentioning and we never heard of anyone getting food poisoning, so we breathed a sigh of relief. For a long time after that if anyone mentioned the word milk Albert would catch my eye and we'd have a quiet snigger.

You wouldn't believe some of the inconveniences we were put to in the early days, especially with most of our runs being in the country with only sparse population. If we'd been carrying factory workers I expect it would have been a different story.

I'm talking about the bridge at Burne midway between Ponte and Selby.

The original stone one must have been a couple of hundred years old and it was just crumbling to bits, unsafe for both cars and pedestrians,

so a wooden footbridge was installed. That meant that we ha͟
one bus between Ponte and Burne and one from the other sia͟͟
Burne and Selby. As a result anyone from the Ponte side of Burne
wanting to go to Selby had to change buses and cross the bridge to do
so. On market days there was a real schemozzle. Most of the passengers
were farmers bringing boxes of eggs, fruit, vegetables, crates of hens,
ducks or rabbits. Since the livestock were carried on the roof of the bus,
at Burne they all had to be hauled down from one bus, carried over the
bridge and loaded on to the roof on the Selby bus.

One time when I was driving the Selby bus everything that could go
wrong did. On the first trip there was a lorry parked right where I
needed to be to unload six crates of ducks and it took us at least ten
minutes to find the driver. That threw me behind schedule right off.

The next trip, one farmer's wife who was bringing eggs to market
swore me down she'd brought five boxes when there were only four. I
had to let her search the bus before she'd admit she'd made a mistake,
but that took another ten minutes. So when I got to Burne for the third
trip I was nearly half an hour late.

I sweated like a bull, climbing up and down, stacking vegetables,
fruit, rabbits and lastly a big crate of hens at the very back. I set off,
hell-for-leather doing at least 35 mph (well above the legal limit), and
there was a strong head wind too which didn't help matters. As soon as
we reached the market the farmers were around me clamouring for
their goods. Down they came, passed from hand to hand till they
reached their rightful owners, rabbits, ducks, the lot, and last of all the
hens.

"Gawd Almighty! Wot the 'ell 'ave yer done to mi 'ens?" I jumped
down and went to investigate. A stocky individual was staring into the
open basket, a scowl of rage on his weatherbeaten face. I went to look.
A pitiful sight!

Enough to make a body weep, anybody but me. I couldn't help it. I
cracked out laughing and so did most of the bystanders who had
crowded around to look.

Those hens were as bare as if they'd been plucked for the oven: just
the combs and a few tail feathers were left. They huddled together
looking downright ashamed of themselves, and no wonder. It was the
wind that had done it of course. That spot at the back of the bus is a
regular wind tunnel and the speed I'd been driving had helped to do a
perfect job of plucking those birds.

"Wot the 'ell am I going to do wi' that lot?" said the farmer, his face beginning to slip a little by now – he had to admit they did look funny.

"You can always label them 'oven ready'," I said as I jumped into the cab and drove away.

You'd think I'd had enough setbacks for one day, but my troubles weren't at an end yet. When we got to the end of that arduous day I made for the café for a final cuppa before we set off for home. The tea was fresh, strong and sweet, just as I liked it and I had a sandwich left. I sat back to relax and enjoy myself, gossiping with my conductress, Iris Gill, and feeling that it wasn't such a bad life after all.

We were thinking of leaving when I felt something nudging my leg. I looked down and there was the Hound of the Baskervilles himself – a magnificent bull mastiff. He put his massive head on my knee and rolled his eyes up at me. He was obviously a friendly animal.

"Hullo, old chap. What do you want?"

I stroked his head.

"I have nothing left for you to eat, old feller, my snap's all gone."

He didn't seem to mind. He just stood there looking at me as if I was his long lost uncle, while I went on stroking him and chatting to him.

Iris looked at her watch.

"Time we were off, 'Arry."

"O.K." I picked up my dust coat and prepared to stand up.

Talk about Dr Jekyll and Mr Hyde! In a flash the gentle friendly animal was transformed into a savage beast. His lip curled, showing gleaming teeth nearly two inches long and from his throat emerged an ominous growl.

I sat down quickly and, at once, he fawned on me again.

"Hey," I said, "I've got to go. I'm not going to hurt you, old chap." Me hurt him! He could have made a meal of me in less time than it takes to tell.

I stood up again, and again he prepared to do me mischief.

I sat down.

"Come on, 'Arry, we're late already."

"How the hell can I? Call this damned dog off, can't you."

"Not me, I'm scared of a toy poodle."

We were in a mess. Every time I tried to get up King Kong was out for my blood. I was getting desperate when a voice called.

"Isn't it time you were off, 'Arry?"

It was Jack Bateson, one of our drivers, grinning all over his face.

"Come on, King," he called and, quiet as a lamb, the dog padded across the floor to him.

"Is that hell-hound yours?" I asked.

"Ay, I just told him to guard you."

If looks could have killed he'd have dropped dead on the spot, but we had a good laugh about it afterwards.

CHAPTER IV

OPERATING PROBLEMS

I think I could write a whole book on this topic, for a more broken-down dilapidated fleet of buses you wouldn't see outside a wrecker's yard. There were three or four Studebakers from the year dot, an Italian model and a few other machines, same era. The few roadworthy models were reserved for the daily Leeds to London run and a monthly run to Brussels. Any of the drivers who had mechanical experience, as I had, were expected to drive the cast-offs. The company I was working for then, 1927, was South Yorkshire Motor Co. and the owner was a Mrs Winder. At the time we thought nothing of it, but looking back it seems a strange business for a woman to be involved in, especially as her husband was a King's Counsel and she probably had no need to work. Perhaps she was ahead of her time and believed women were as capable as men at running a business, but she certainly didn't look like a typical feminist; she was a bit like the Queen Mum in appearance and she had a warm smile and a kind word for all her employees. What is more to the point she paid well and those of us who had to drive the real wrecks got five shillings a week extra.

Having done that, however, she seemed to think her responsibility was at an end, for not a penny was spent on the upkeep of those buses except in cases of dire emergency.

As I said, I could write a whole book on the mechanical problems, but it would be pretty boring for a layman to read so I'll just confine myself to the more interesting of our efforts to keep the buses on the road. Take those leaking radiators:

People living on the bus route must have got sick of seeing us coming to the door, bucket in hand.

"Could you let us have a bucket of water, missus? Radiator's leaking."

"What, again? Come on 'and it over and try not to come again. My 'usband's on nights and I don't want to wake 'im." Smiling gratefully, but cursing inwardly I took the bucket and filled the radiator.

One day on the way to Doncaster I must have stopped half a dozen times and I was nearly at the end of my tether, and then when I got to Norton, about nine miles from Doncaster, I had a brainwave. I stopped outside a grocer's shop and beckoned Cyril, my conductor, to the front.

"What's up?" he said.

"Give us a couple o' bob," I said. "I've had a bright idea."

"Look after it, it must be mighty lonely," he said with a grin but he counted out two shillings in pennies.

I picked up the ever-handy bucket and dashed into the shop.

"Got any packets of soup, missus?" I asked the plump smiling woman behind the counter.

"Aye lad, but you can't eat it like that. It 'as to be cooked, and I've never yet seen a bus with a kitchen on it."

"I'll cook it alright," I said mysteriously. "Give me a dozen and a bucket of water, please."

She still looked doubtful, but she handed over the packets and filled the bucket.

I should explain about packet soups: they were nothing more than flour (or some kind of thickening) and synthetic flavours, but they had fancy names, oxtail, mock turtle, mulligatawny and when you'd added water and boiled it for a while, you had a tasty bowl of soup, filling, but not very nourishing – poor folk's substitute for a square meal.

I ran back to the bus, took off the radiator cap, tore open the soup packets and shook the contents of each one into the hole, poured in the bucket of water, gave Cyril the nod, jumped into the cab and started up the motor. We had lost quite a bit of time but I managed to make it up and drove into Doncaster bus depot practically on time. By now the water in the radiator was well and truly on the boil and a delicious, savoury smell was filling the air. Passengers waiting for the bus began sniffing and looking round curiously.

"There must be a café somewhere," I heard one woman remark, "but I don't know where it could be. Do you?" she asked her companion.

"Nearest one's on Yates Street, but you couldn't smell that from here," was the reply, "and anyway they never 'ad owt that smelt as good as this."

I nudged Cyril, who had come round to the cab for a moment and was in on the secret by now.

"By gum 'Arry, what are you up to now – operating a soup kitchen?" One of our regular customers, a burly red-cheeked farmer came up to us. I told him what I'd done and I thought he'd never stop laughing. He gave me a slap on the shoulder that nearly sent me flying.

"I'll say this for thee, 'Arry lad, tha' never sticks fast – tho' mebbe t' engine will. I must tell the missus about this." He climbed on to the bus still chuckling.

We drew quite a bit of attention on our way to Thorpe Audlin and Cyril swears that when we stopped outside one of the cottages on the way, a woman came to the door with a bowl in her hand, looking up and down the lane to see where the smell was coming from. Anyway that soup lasted all the way back to Doncaster without needing a refill and for two or three days after we only had to fill up at the depot.

But however annoying the leaking radiators were, at least they were child's play compared with brake problems. Not one of the machines we drove had reliable brakes and we all carried a can of brake fluid at all times.

One Sunday I was coming out of Little Smeaton towards Wentbridge and down Bluebell Hill, which has a gradient of one in five and sometimes one in three, when the brakes failed. Frantically I pumped on the brake pedal.

"Come on, come on, you bastard," I growled. Nothing doing. I was fast approaching the main road and there was an A.A. man at the bottom directing traffic. He held up his hand for me to stop. Fat chance! With both hands I signalled to him to move away and he jumped clear just in time.

What a predicament! This was Sunday afternoon in the early summer. Brock o' Dale woods on the outskirts of Wentbridge – at this time of year a sea of bluebells – was a favourite haunt of picnickers and it seemed then as if the world and his wife and his family were out enjoying the sunshine. I kept pumping the brakes, although I knew it was a lost cause. We were going too fast to apply the handbrake and it was too dangerous to get into a lower gear. The bus gathered momentum. We were doing at least 40 mph and a quarter of a mile further on

I needed to turn left – what a hope! The only thing I could do was to keep on going until the road levelled off – so on I went horn blaring and praying that no one would try to cross the road suddenly. I must have aged ten years in those few minutes.

At last – level ground and then a gentle climb – slower and slower and then I was able to ease the bus into the edge of the pavement, gradually manoeuvre it into a turn and make my way back to the depot.

There was no mechanic on duty, it being Sunday, so I filled the bus up with brake fluid and then went into the office. Mrs Winder was there so I told her what had happened.

"Oh, I'm so sorry, Mr Jordan." (Mr Jordan. I was all of eighteen!) "I am going to have all the machines overhauled I promise you – and thank you for managing so well."

I made a few sounds like, "Don't mention it. It was no trouble." – She always overwhelmed me.

"Now, do you think you could manage to drive it as far as Pontefract and back? The London bus should be in by then and you can take that for the rest of the shift."

What else could I do but agree. At least there were no more hills and the town would be quiet with the shops closed. So on I went, and on and on. There was no one there when I got back to the depot and no London bus in sight. I drove the rest of the shift very, very carefully, checking the brakes and adding brake fluid every few miles and returned to the depot at 11 p.m. feeling as if I'd been through a wringer – several times. Mrs Winder was there when I got back and she thanked me profusely for doing so well. She also assured me again all the buses were going to be done over. I don't recollect that ever happening.

Another problem was dirt in the carburettor. There were no air filters in those days and over the years gravel, dirt, bits of rubber and moisture accumulated in the bottom of the petrol tank and as it was sucked up into the carburettor caused it to backfire repeatedly and quite often stopped the engine altogether. Out I would get, swing the starter handle and get it going again. Sometimes that wouldn't be enough and I had to open the hood, swing the engine, dash round to get to the accelerator rod, lift it up and down until the engine started, then get back into the cab before the engine died on me again.

On the 6:30 a.m. bus from Thorpe Audlin to Askern we had a regular passenger and often the only one, an elderly man who was in charge of the pit ponies at Askern colliery. I'd had carburettor trouble ever since I left the depot and before long I had to go through the usual process, but this time the engine stalled every time before I got back into the cab. Finally I went up to the passenger.

"Can you give us a hand, Sam?" I asked.

"Sure, lad. What is it?"

He climbed out of the bus and followed me to the front. When he saw the hood open he stopped. "Nay, lad – I know nowt about engines."

"You don't need to know anything," I said. "You see this lever? As soon as the engine starts just lift it up a quarter of an inch and hold it."

As gingerly as if he were approaching a stick of dynamite he reached forward and lifted the rod. I swung the handle and the engine started. Bang! The carburettor backfired and a flame four to five inches long shot out.

"Bloody 'ell!" Sam sprang back several feet.

"Tha'll 'ave to do it thissen lad or else find somebody else. I might 'ave 'ad me 'and blown off."

I tried coaxing. I tried reasoning to no avail. At last he said, "I know what I will do." He walked over to a nearby tree and broke off a branch about six feet long.

"I'll do it wi'this."

I couldn't help laughing.

"Nay, Sam, you'd break t' accelerator rod. No, we'll just have to sit here and wait for a car to come by – if we're lucky, or the next bus an hour later."

We were on a quiet country road and vehicles were few and far between. It would have been useless to walk to the nearest house, about two miles away. They wouldn't have a phone – nobody had in those days.

Sam was deep in thought.

"By gow, lad, I've got an idea."

He opened the gate into a nearby field where three or four horses were grazing. He put his fingers in his mouth and gave a shrill whistle; he repeated this a few times in different cadences. At once the horses came trotting towards him, nuzzling him and receiving pats and encouraging words from him. Gradually he separated one horse from the rest and with surprising agility leapt onto his back – no saddle, no reins – nothing!

"Shut t' gate, 'Arry," he said. "I'll not be long. I'm off to t' depot to
tell 'em to send another bus."

And like a knight on his charger riding to the rescue he galloped off
the way we'd come.

There was nothing to be done now, but wait to see what happened. I
sat in the bus and ate some of my snap (lunch) and sure enough, about
twenty minutes later a relief bus arrived and, close behind, Sir Galahad
on his trusty steed.

It wasn't always the condition of the buses that gave us problems;
sometimes the elements lent a helping hand. Autumn of 1928 was one
of the wettest on record. England is not noted for its sunny weather,
but I swear we never once saw the sun from January to September.
All this wet only aggravated the usual problems: mainly water in
the carburettor, more backfiring and engines stalling. Windshields
streamed with water and wipers were primitive in the extreme. The
route from Pontefract to Askern was a very circuitous one, from one
small village or town after another, places like Ferrybridge, Cridling
Stubbs, Little Smeaton, Askern and Bentley. One afternoon as I drove
through the country area I was perturbed to see most of the fields, at
either side of the road, standing in water and many ditches flooding
over, but by the time I returned by the same route it was dark and in
the headlights I could see water surging over the road like the tide
coming in. It would have been up to the wheel arches if I'd carried on.
I braked cautiously, put the bus into reverse and backed onto higher
ground, turned round and made my way to the main Doncaster road
and went back the direct route, missing all my regular stops. It wasn't
until the next day I realised what a narrow escape I'd had. The river
Don had overflowed its banks and villages for miles around were
almost completely submerged. Families were evacuated by boat, leaving most of their belongings behind. Some refused to leave and supplies
were brought to them by boat and handed in through the bedroom
windows – no helicopters to drop supplies or make rescues in those
days.

It wasn't until two months later that the country service was restored
and we heard that the government had had to bring in experts from
Holland to help control the floods. The state of those homes in the
flooded areas was pitiful to see: sodden couches, beds and bedclothes,
broken chairs and tables stacked on the front lawns, people making

pathetic attempts to clean out the mud and repair furniture where possible. There was a Flood Relief Fund set up sponsored by the government and as always in times like that friends and neighbours rallied round and gave time, money and goods to help the stricken countryside.

Nowadays when catastrophes all over the world reach us the moment they occur, we seem to have become almost hardened to seeing harrowing sights, but then we only knew what we experienced ourselves and I'll tell you, the effect of those floods was devastating on all of us.

Rain was always with us and except in such extreme cases didn't create much of a problem, but fog was an entirely different matter and I don't think there was a man among us who didn't dread driving in the fog.

I know much has been done to eradicate most of the causes of heavy fogs, but then, with collieries, factories and private houses pouring thick smoke into the air, there's no wonder fogs were almost impenetrable. The clouds which hung over the North Country ten months of the year seemed to delight in descending and mating with the smoke, encircling every particle of soot with a drop of moisture. Try blowing your nose on one of those days and you'd swear your handkerchief had been used to wipe the fireback.

Needless to say it was hell on earth to try and drive a bus on one of those days. Schedules went by the board; passengers were thankful to see a bus at all. Many times the conductors had to walk on the kerb just ahead of the bus to show the driver the way and even then they had to take care to stay close to the bus or they would get lost in the fog.

My most terrifying experience happened in the mid-1930s. A lot of changes had taken place by then. E.P. Bullock of Bullock Brothers had bought the business from Mrs Winder and much had been done to bring the fleet up to scratch. Not that they were much to write home about even then, but we long-time drivers appreciated the improvements. The depot had been moved to Pontefract so I didn't have as far to go to get to work and I now had a motorbike – the apple of my eye. But when I woke up that morning and saw the fog I knew I'd have all on to get to work on time; my bus was due out at 6:30 a.m.

It seemed as if I was the only person alive as I mounted my bike and rode very, very cautiously along the street; every sound was muffled and when another person loomed out of the dense fog he seemed to be magnified to twice the normal size. I'd been that way hundreds of times but I suddenly found myself on the wrong side of the road when I came to an intersection. I rode diagonally across it instead of turning left. I thought I was going straight and wondered why the centre line was suddenly turning to the right. Well, I got to work without mishap and managed to get the bus on the stand and metaphorically girded up my loins for the long day ahead.

There were only a few passengers, mostly miners on the early shift, and they didn't seem to mind how long we took to get there. At least they would be able to see the way when they got underground. A woman in the front seat was of the nervous type; she kept peering out of the window.

"Are you sure it's safe to drive in the fog?" she asked. "You can't see your 'and in front of your face."

"Sure it's safe, missus. I know this route like the back of me 'and," I said, but it had a hollow ring to it. She was only going as far as East Hardwicke, which was just as well or she'd have had her worst fears come true if she'd gone any further.

Soon after that I was on the main Doncaster road and there were a few more vehicles on the road, all creeping along at two or three miles an hour, but you didn't see them till they were nearly on top of you. Headlights were useless; all they did was illuminate that heavy grey blanket and throw back a reflection that was even more impenetrable. There were no sounds above the engine noise and suddenly it was upon me – on my side of the road and coming straight for me – a lorry loaded with steel girders. Adrenalin flowing, with a superhuman effort I wrenched the steering wheel round and drove into the ditch. I was almost too late. With a resounding crunch and crash of shattered glass some of those girders ripped through my side of the cab and the side windows of the bus. Fortunately, I had placed the bus at an angle by driving into the ditch. The passengers had been flung to the side farthest from the smash and no one was hurt, but one girder must have missed me by inches.

There was an almost deafening silence for several seconds; then one by one with loud groans and even louder curses the passengers sorted themselves out. I clawed my way out of the cab through the space made by the girder then went round to the door of the bus to help the passengers alight. We stood gazing in wonder at the wreckage – wonder that we had all escaped unharmed.

Just then a figure loomed out of the fog. He had been following us in a lorry at a safe distance and had heard the crash.

"It's a good job I warn't any nearer or I might 'ave been in t' crash as well. I'd best go get t' police. It's only about 'alf a mile away."

He returned shortly and the police set to work taking statements, measuring skid marks and assessing damages.

I knew the sergeant and he came over to take my statement.

"I think you'd better know, 'Arry, that he says you're to blame."

"Bloody 'ell! What the heck am I supposed to have done?"

"He says you drove into him and dragged his lorry across to this side of the road."

This was adding insult to injury. I nearly exploded – then I saw he was grinning.

"Don't worry,lad. We've plenty of evidence: skid marks, the angle of the crash, the evidence of your passengers. There's no doubt he was to blame."

And at the Magistrates' Court in Pontefract a couple of weeks later, police evidence exonerated me of all blame. The lorry driver's licence was suspended for three years and his firm had to pay all costs.

CHAPTER V

GROWING PAINS

What tremendous changes have taken place in the transport business since I started over sixty years ago. Practically everyone has what Roosevelt promised – "a car in every garage" – only now it's more often two or even three. Bus-riding is now almost luxurious especially on coach tours, and underground trains in many areas do much to facilitate getting from A to B.

When I started in 1923 buses had solid tyres and that, plus cobbled streets, made bus-riding a bone-shaking experience. Many times the windshield vibrated so much that visibility was almost nil. The windshields opened in those days; they were hinged across the top and could be opened at the bottom by means of wing nuts and swung ajar three or four inches. Then you had to crouch down in the seat in order to see out of the gaps and when it rained – watch out!

Anyone who wanted to start a bus company only had to have enough capital to buy a few buses, then work out a timetable to service certain areas and, provided the drivers had licences and obeyed the road laws, there was no one to say them nay.

There was a good deal of piracy going on. Somebody else could start up in opposition and steal the other company's passengers. I, personally, knew a group of miners who did just that. Ten of them clubbed together and bought a second-hand bus. Then they got hold of a Bullock's timetable and arrived at the bus-stops five or ten minutes before the regular bus and picked up any waiting passengers. We tried to get ahead of them, but we were handicapped by having to stick to the timetable. There was a lot of hard feelings about this piracy – if takings went down a considerable amount, the company was unable to pay full wages. They sabotaged the buses in other ways: when they found one unattended, perhaps the driver and conductor were on a lunch break, they put sugar in the petrol tank and took the carbide out of the lights. We had to be on our toes all the time.

Trams gave us quite a bit of competition, but of course they were confined to roads where there were tracks and they, the tram tracks, were another bugbear. Add them to the cobbled streets and solid tyres and you had an even bumpier ride.

There was a lot of horse traffic, of course, mostly brewers' drays, and if you got behind one of those you could count on being several minutes behind schedule. Horses were very leery of motor vehicles and when the bus backfired, as it frequently did, I've seen a horse turn round and take off in the opposite direction, the dray bumping behind it at maybe ten miles an hour, the driver pulling on the reins and cracking his whip to try and stop the terrified animal. Usually though he would pull over and let us pass, get down, hold the reins and soothe the horse until we got by.

In spite of all these obstacles bus companies were beginning to present quite a bit of competition to the railway companies and they didn't like it one bit. L.M.S. and L.N.E.R., the two most powerful companies began to lobby the government to bring in stiffer laws to reduce the competition from road transport and in 1930 the Road and Rail Traffic Act came into being. The Ministry of Transport appointed Inspectors to make sure everyone conformed and they examined everything from the roadworthiness of the buses to the punctuality of the services, and the number of standing passengers allowed to the strict observance of the Highway Code, which by the way had not even been published. Everywhere you went these government spies were trying to catch you out. On one occasion as I was turning a corner the petrol washed up to the filter cap and a thin stream spilled out of the tiny air-hole at the top and trickled onto the road. An inspector standing on the corner saw this, came over to where I was picking up passengers and gave me a notice ordering the bus to be taken off the road until the leak had been rectified.

We drivers did get some benefits from this stricter legislation: the condition of the vehicles improved by at least eighty per cent, but we still resented this continued surveillance. The final straw came when all drivers were compelled to take a test proving we were competent to drive a Public Service Vehicle. Most of us had been driving for at least five years and thought we knew all there was to know about bus driving. How wrong we were!

There were fourteen of us to take the test and we went in one of the company's buses, to Leeds City Hall. It was sometime in October, a grey, rainy day – typically English, and we were all feeling a bit nervous. Not a lot – after all we knew how to drive and we knew the rules of the road. What we didn't know was the kind of person who was going to do the examining. We were all assembled in the waiting room when he marched in. A retired army officer by the looks of him, used to licking rookies into shape and all gung-ho to do the same with a set of country bumpkins who thought they could drive.

"You!" he snapped pointing to Mike Johnson. "Fetch the bus round to the main door – on the double." Mike looked stunned for a moment then got to his feet and hesitated.

"Get a move on! We haven't got all day." Mike wasted no more time.

"You lot wait here and don't make a nuisance of yourselves."

We were all too flabbergasted to talk for a few minutes – then "Oo the 'ell does 'e think 'e is?" asked Billy Evans.

"Anybody'd think we were in the ruddy army."

"I'll tell 'im where 'e gets off if he starts talking to me like that!"

We all had plenty to say, but we knew we'd have to grin and bear it. Driving examiners were usually a bit unapproachable, but not as bad as this one.

In about fifteen minutes Mike came in, obviously shaken, but trying to grin. We wanted to ask him how he got on. No chance! The martinet marched him off down some steps and, as we found out later, put him in a little cubicle in the cellar with strict instructions to stay there and not try to talk to anyone. There wasn't going to be a single loophole, not a vestige of opportunity to cheat on this exam.

It was my turn next and I certainly wasn't looking forward to it, but to my surprise as soon as we got on the bus, me in the cab and the examiner at the conductor's window, he became quite friendly.

"My name's Thornton," he said. "What's yours?"

Of course I told him, then started up the engine and waited for instructions.

"Just ease into the traffic," he said, "and carry on until I tell you to turn. How long have you been driving, Jordan?" he asked as I drove along. "You seem very young to have been driving all that time. Take a right here," he said suddenly – and left me to cope with a stream of on-coming traffic and a load of vehicles backed up behind me. I stuck my hand out and finally managed to ease my way into the intersection and carried on, now on a tram route.

"Do you come to Leeds often?" was his next query. "I don't mean when you're on duty, but just for a night out. If you do, try that pub on your left, just behind the Grand. Can you see it? It's called the Crown and Anchor." I ignored him. I kept my eyes glued on the road and the oncoming traffic. I'd tumbled to his game and wasn't going to be led astray by his pseudo-friendliness. That was the most exhausting, nerve-racking twenty minutes of my whole driving career. He took me through the busiest streets and gave me last minute instructions which barely gave me time to change gear. At one point when we were right up to an intersection he rapped out, "Turn left here." My blood was boiling by this time. I felt no test was worth all this aggravation. I passed the intersection, pulled into the kerb and stopped the bus.

"What kind of a B.F. would expect me to turn left with no warning, no chance to signal or check on-coming traffic?"

He put his hand through the window and patted my shoulder.

"It's O.K., lad. You did the right thing. Now we'd better get back. I've twelve more people to examine."

He didn't give me any more instructions. I knew the way and just drove with due care and attention, thankful it was over. Then when we were half way back a funeral cortege pulled out just ahead of us. The traffic slowed to a crawl and the pavement at each side became thronged with spectators – it must have been someone important.

Thornton began to show signs of impatience.

"We'll never get back at this rate. Can't you pull ahead? You could just get between that tram and the hearse. Go on, I won't dock you any marks."

He was talking to deaf ears. I was taking no chances, not after all he'd put me through.

We got back eventually and I was sent to my little cubicle to while away the time as best I could. One by one the others joined us in their assigned cubicles and then we were taken back upstairs and given a written test.

We were a fairly cheerful group who made our way back to Pontefract that evening. Eleven out of the fourteen had passed; but that didn't mean that the three who failed were bad drivers. I think they had been taken in by Thornton's trickery and failed to remember the essential rule of driving, "Keep you eye and your mind on the job and never assume that the other chap will do likewise."

In the long run it was the bus companies who benefited from all this legislation. Buses became more roadworthy and as a consequence drivers were able to concentrate on driving without worrying about possible breakdowns. Passengers began to appreciate the greater advantage of road as opposed to rail travel. They rarely had to walk as far to a bus-stop as they had to a railway station and before long bus companies had the monopoly of passenger transport.

CHAPTER VI

CHARTER BUSES

Before World War II holidays with pay were the exception rather than the rule, so for many people an occasional day trip to the seaside was the only holiday they got, and for that they hired a bus or, in the very early days, a charabanc. A 'chara' as it was usually called was a favourite with many people, and on a sunny day riding along country roads and open woodland, watching the world go by, was an exciting experience, especially as the occasions were few and far between. But English weather being what it is, however sunny it was when the party started out, clouds would be sure to gather and rain begin to fall. There was a canvas cover, of course, and a framework to support it, but half the fun of the trip was gone when you were shut up and a lot of the view shut out. Now the organizers of the trip had to prove their worth: get a sing-song going, get the children playing a game – who could count the most cows, horses, sheep or whatever – bring out picnic baskets and sweets. To give them their due the holiday-makers were usually easily pleased and determined to enjoy themselves no matter what. If the trip was to the seaside – Blackpool, Bridlington or Scarborough – and it was necessary to stop halfway, arrangements would have been made ahead of time at a halfway house and here the grown-ups could get cups of tea and buns, the children ice-cream and pop. This was part of the treat, as grown-ups rarely, and children never, went into cafés in these days. Eventually the three or four hour trip would end and everyone came tumbling out to get a first sight of the sea; but I liked to watch the wonder dawning on the faces of children used to being surrounded by bricks and mortar, as they got their first glimpse of the limitless expanse of sand and sea. Then there was a mad rush for the sands, buckets and spades at the ready, shoes and socks removed for paddling and, if they had a penny, there were donkey rides along the beach.

Most of us enjoyed taking charters, none of the stopping and starting of city driving. Much of the journey was on quiet country roads, and this was long before the bumper to bumper driving we endure now. When we got to our destination we were free to do what we liked and were paid half-rate for doing it. Of course we had to see the bus was safely parked and keep going back to it periodically in case some of the passengers wanted to get back on. This happened sometimes when it rained although there were amusement parks and shops in abundance and shelters on the promenade. If I was on my own I usually filled the time by going for walks. When you were cooped up in a bus all your working day it was a treat to get some exercise. We got a free meal at the café the party patronized; most of us went for fish and chips – fresh fish then and not off a refrigerator ship and several weeks old.

Sometimes two or three buses were needed and then we had someone to pal around with when we arrived. In some ways this was unfortunate as most of us were quite young and eager for a lark. One of our favourite pranks was to drive the bus along the promenade and, when you got to a spot where the place was packed with trippers and dozens of seagulls were circling overhead looking for scraps, you turned the ignition off, pressed the accelerator and then turned the ignition on again. There would be a tremendous bang as the engine backfired and the seagulls, scared to death, showered blessings from on high on the luckless trippers.

We didn't do things like that very often. Mostly, if it was a nice day, we'd be satisfied to go for walks or sit on the sands watching the sea and the kids.

Those were ordinary charters where the party just wanted to get to the destination, spend the day as they pleased and then come back at six or seven in the evening, but they *had* reserved the bus from say 7 a.m. until 10 p.m. and were entitled to make use of it whenever they wished. I remember one such party as if it were yesterday.

It was a party of women from Featherstone Square, a place notorious in those days for the riff-raff who lived there. I don't want to sound like a snob – I'm just a common working man and never pretended to be anything else – but they were the dregs of humanity and when I heard that they had chartered a bus and I was to drive them I nearly went spare. I tried to get a replacement who would take it. No dice! Everybody had heard of them. I was due to pick them up at the Jubilee Hotel in Featherstone at 7 a.m. and, as I caught sight of that gaggle of harridans loud in both dress and speech, I nearly quit the job, regardless of the consequences, but then I thought, "They'll be in the bus, I'll be in the cab and once we get to Cleethorpes, I'll be rid of them until time to come back." That's what I thought; this is what happened.

They crowded onto the bus, not without a lot of back chat.

"You'll take care of us luv, won't you?" – to me.

"Eeh 'e's a lovely feller in't 'e."

"Can I come in't cab wi' you?"

I tried to ignore them but it wasn't easy. The last two came out of the pub, followed by a couple of barmen each carrying four cases of beer, two dozen in each, which they stacked in the aisle. Then I began to get some inkling of what the day would be like. I drove along to Pontefract, Knottingley, Goole with my cargo yelling, cackling, singing bawdy songs and drawing the attention of every passerby. Periodically one of them would come and slide my window open and offer me a bottle of beer. I tried to refuse, but in the end for the sake of peace and quiet I took one and put it on the floor. I prayed for the journey to end and drove as fast as I dared.

When we got to Goole there was a hold-up on the railway bridge. A sergeant and police constable were stopping oncoming traffic because of an accident on the bridge. The constable came over to me.

"It won't be long, driver, the towaway truck is here already and they'll soon be finished."

My cargo didn't care how long it was; they wanted to be in on the action. They began climbing out of the bus and wandering, not too steadily, towards the accident. Two or three of them made a bee-line for the cop.

"Ooh don't you just love a bobby?" said one.

"'E's so big and strong – let's feel your muscles love."

The first one didn't like that.

"Keep your 'ands off," she said. "I saw 'im first."

The embarrassed constable tried to assert his authority.

"You can't go up there, madam, ladies," he called. "Will you please get back on the bus?"

"I do love a masterful man," cooed another lady admiringly.

The sergeant was now in on the action stemming the flow of thrill seekers intent on getting a ringside seat. He was a big, burly man with a face like a bruiser and much more accustomed to command than the unfortunate bobby.

"Move along there, missus. You, madam, you can't go there. Get back into the bus the lot of you if you don't want a summons for obstructing a police officer." This threat had the desired effect. I got the impression that this wasn't the first time some of them had had a brush with the law.

The sergeant confirmed this when he strolled over to me after they'd all got back in the bus.

"I wouldn't like to be in your shoes, driver," he said. "Where are you off to?"

I told him Cleethorpes.

"Well, I wish you joy of 'em. There's one or two there who have already seen the inside of a prison cell. Good luck."

I managed to get to Cleethorpes without further mishap. We had run into rain a few miles from the coast and now it was throwing it down. I drove to the parking lot and went inside the bus to find out where they wanted to go. Most of them were well away by then and couldn't care less about the rain. I spoke to a Mrs Briggs who was in charge of the party and was soberer than the others.

"That's alright, driver. We're going to a meeting of the Working Women's Guild at the Elephant and Castle and we'll probably get a meal there. You can join us if you like about four o'clock."

"No, no thank you," I said hastily. "I have to keep an eye on the bus. I'll get some fish and chips at one of the shops on the promenade."

I drove them to the hotel and told Mrs Briggs I'd pick them up at six o'clock sharp.

The rest of the day was one of unmitigated boredom for me, but at least I was shot of my cargo for a few hours. I was at the Elephant and Castle at six o'clock and went inside to collect them, and as I suspected they'd been having a merry old time and I'd like to bet that the only meeting that had taken place had been between mouths and beer bottles.

In twos and threes they staggered into the bus and collapsed onto the seats. "Good," I thought. "They won't be long before they're asleep and we'll be home in four hours." What a hope ! We hadn't been driving for half an hour when they began rapping on the window. I slid it open. "What now?"

"There's a pub just ahead, driver. How about us going in for a quick one?"

"Don't you think you've had enough?"

Mrs Briggs spoke up. "We've chartered this bus, we're paying for it and you, so shut your trap and pull over." She was in the right, of course, so I had no alternative but to stop. However, I gave them a stern warning.

"Seven-thirty – no later – or I go without you. We'll not be back by ten as it is. Anybody not out by seven-thirty gets left behind."

They saw I meant it and rushed off to get some much needed refreshment!

The next leg of the journey was the worst; we hadn't gone many miles after leaving the pub when I realized I was lost. It was shortly after World War II when many signposts had been removed or turned around in case of invasion, especially in coastal areas. Unfortunately, many of them had not yet been replaced. When I got back on the road after we left the pub I missed the turn-off to Goole. I soon realized my error, but now which way to go? Fortunately for me I saw a farmhouse ahead and a farmer driving his tractor in the field. I stopped the bus and ran across to ask him for directions. He only took a matter of minutes to set me right, but the damage had been done. My flock, eager to be rid of all the beer they'd drunk, came trooping after me and spying a privy at the back of the house made a bee-line for it. You can imagine the havoc they wreaked in that quiet farmyard: some of them couldn't wait their turn at the privy, but squatted down behind the barn or among haystacks. Fortunately, it had stopped raining and the sun was beginning to show.

The farmer stood there, a grim look on his face and I was feeling even angrier, but what could two males do among a crowd of women, and such women.

"I'll thank you never to come here again, driver," he said when at last they were all on the bus.

And now we were on the last leg of the journey, only about forty miles to go, no more calls of nature to answer and a drunken sleep beginning to overcome the passengers. The sun sank over the horizon, a few stars became visible, lights began to appear in cottages we passed and street lights came on – peace prevailed.

A few passengers who were awake began singing 'Roll out the barrel' quite quietly, but loud enough to rouse more people. As the singing became louder, some voices were raised in anger at being wakened; then another voice,

"It's only nine o'clock. 'Ow far 'ave we to go?"

One of them opened my window.

"'Ow far 'ave we to go driver?"

"About ten miles," I said shortly.

"Did you 'ear that girls? Only ten miles to go, we've time to stop for a quick one." She turned to me again.

"Stop at the next pub, will you,lad? We'll not stay long."

There was nothing else for it and so I pulled up and resigned myself to the inevitable. They were too far gone to be satisfied with one or two drinks and it was closing time before they finally directed their wavering footsteps towards the bus and I didn't get to Featherstone until eleven o'clock. I swore to myself, "Never again. I'll quit first."

An entirely different tour was one chartered by the Ladies Social Club from Featherstone church. This time it was to Whitby. It was a nice day and the road led over the Yorkshire Moors and revealed some spectacular views. All went well until the road started to climb and the old bus began to falter. I changed down and dropped the speed to about fifteen mph, and all went well for a while until we came to Bransby Bank where the gradient was one in three. There was no way the old machine was going to make it. I drew into the grass verge, stopped and went into the bus.

"I'm sorry, ladies," I said. "I have to ask you to get out and walk up the hill; otherwise the bus won't make it."

Without a word of complaint they all climbed out; a few of them even offered to give me a push.

I laughed.

"Oh, no. That won't be necessary, but I'm obliged to you just the same."

They made almost as good time as I did and some of them were halfway up before I passed them. They waved and some of them cheered as the bus went by.

There were no more hold-ups and we reached Whitby in good time. We arranged where and when I should pick them up and we went our separate ways.

When I arrived at our meeting place at six o'clock, Mrs Ross, who was in charge of the party, approached me.

"When we get to Bransby Bank, driver, we've decided we'd rather walk than be driven down that steep hill. Some of the ladies feel a bit nervous about it."

"You'll be perfectly safe," I assured her. "I'll drive at two miles an hour if that will make you feel better."

But I couldn't persuade them and dutifully stopped at the top of the hill and let them off.

The rest of the journey was without incident. They took up a collection for me, which was usual for charter drivers, and a very good one it was. I dropped them off in groups of three or four near to where they lived. The last one to leave was Mrs Ross and I stopped outside the tobacconist's shop which she and her husband owned. As I came round to the door to help her off she said, "Just come into the shop a minute, will you?" Mystified I followed her and watched her get a ladder, place it against the shelves and climb to the top one. She came down with two packs of cigarettes in her hand. "I hope you'll accept these young man as a thank you for the care you took of us. We had a lovely day."

"Thank you, missus. Thank you very much," I added as I looked at the packets. They were 'Sarony Silk-Cut', the most expensive cigarettes you could buy then.

I lit up as soon as I got back into the cab. What a shock! They must have been in the shop for twenty years. It set me off coughing so much that I nearly choked. I threw the cigarette out of the window. When I got to the garage I opened both packs. The contents were green with mould! I'm sure the old dear had no idea; there wouldn't have been any demand for them in the years of the depression and they had probably been there since the shop was opened.

The worst charter I ever took was a group of officials of the Yorkshire Miners' Association. They were going to a convention in Whitby. A Colonel Hargreaves was in charge and they were all big shots on the Coal Board, but the fault didn't lie with them; it was the bus. I found out later – too late – that another driver had taken the bus I should have had. We set out from Ackworth and before we got to Ferrybridge the bus broke down. This was after the war, but buses still didn't have air or petrol filters and consequently bits of rubber and grit had collected in the carburettor plugging it. I took out the main jet, blew it clean and set off again. Less than three miles further on it happened again and this time I phoned the S.Y. office and told them to bring another bus; this was in no state to get to Whitby and back.

Half an hour later the chief mechanic arrived, but in the break-down truck as there wasn't a bus available.

He did what I did, more or less, only with better equipment and I set off again. They followed me for about two miles and then left me, just before it all happened again. Colonel Hargreaves came out to see what was going on. I knew him quite well as he often travelled on my bus, so I could let off steam a bit and I also apologized profusely.

"It's not your fault, lad," he said. "They'd no right to send such a broken-down vehicle. I'll have something to say to Reg when we get back." (Reg was E.P. Bullock's son.) "But in the meantime what are you going to do?"

"I'll just have to phone again and this time I'll tell them they've got to send another bus." I stressed the poor condition of the bus, told them there was sludge coming out of the main tank and it was vital that they bring another bus. I was now twelve miles on my way and it had taken two hours to get there.

I waited impatiently for nearly half an hour before rescue came in the shape of the same break-down bus, but they had brought a new tank and jets and thirty gallons of petrol. They took about fifteen minutes to replace the tank and once more followed me for a couple of miles before turning back and then – you wouldn't believe it, I couldn't – the bus broke down again.

The air in the cab was blue with all the words I used to describe the bus, the mechanics and South Yorkshire Motors *in toto*. Then I got out to see what was wrong. The tube from the carburettor into the manifold was missing. The mechanic had obviously been in such a hurry to get the job done, he hadn't secured it properly and it had fallen out. I walked back the way we had come, trying to find it, but there was no sign of it; it could have rolled into the ditch or got lost in the grass verge. I was wasting my time. I got back in the bus and managed to get it going, albeit very slowly. About two hundred yards ahead I came to a garage and pulled in to see if they could provide me with another tube. It wasn't equipped for bus work but I did manage to find a tube which was not quite long enough, so I fixed it into position with some electrician's tape. It did enable the carburettor to pump petrol into the engine, but only very slowly and I managed to drive the remaining fifty-odd miles, but very, very slowly.

We reached Whitby at 6 p.m., too late for the Colliery Board meeting, almost too late for anything except to get back to Ackworth.

Colonel Hargreaves approached me.

"We've decided to have a brief meeting among ourselves and then have a quick meal. I'll tell the manager to see you get a good meal. You deserve one and I'm sure you need one. We'll meet you in the parking lot at 7 p.m. And, incidentally, I'm going to phone Reg from the hotel and tell him what I think of his buses, but I'll also compliment him on having such an efficient driver."

He gave me a quick pat on the shoulder and got back in the bus.

We set off back at 7 p.m. and arrived at Ackworth 12 p.m.

CHAPTER VII

ME AND THE LAW

I don't want you to be misled by the title of this chapter. I was never in trouble with the law, quite the contrary. In those days the police and transport drivers often worked together, perhaps more so than they do now. As a matter of fact I seriously thought of joining the police force, partly to escape from the monotony of bus driving and partly for the excitement. In those days I think there was more excitement and far less danger in being a bobby than there is now. Finally, I took the plunge and applied for a position with Leeds City Police Force. I had to go and have an examination both physical and written. I didn't expect to have any problems with the physical – I was tall and broad and exercised regularly – but was pleased to know that I did quite well on the written test. I didn't find that out at the time, of course; they said they'd "let me know".

Not content with one application, however, I also applied to Bradford City and the West Riding and went through similar examinations. I was quite flabbergasted when I was accepted by all three, but there was a fly in the ointment and a big one at that. Though there was only a few shillings difference in the starting pay at each place, the highest pay was 15 shillings a week less than I was getting as a bus driver and the hours were worse. I know I could have retired on a pension in twenty-five years time but when you are only twenty-three, twenty-five years is an awful long time to wait. I decided to stick with the bus driving.

One of the occasions when we were glad to see 'the men in blue' was after a race meeting. Pontefract had a fairly important racecourse and well-known racehorse owners from many parts of England would gather there, followed by the usual hangers-on, tic-tac men, book-makers, gamblers, small time and big time. After the races were over they would all congregate, winners and losers, in Pontefract's many pubs. At one time there were fifty-two, the Gardeners Arms, the Crown, the Robin Hood, the New Inn, the Red Lion, the Turk's Head, to name only a few. And at closing time you could imagine what a scramble there was to catch the late buses to Leeds or Doncaster; there was very little overnight accommodation in Pontefract.

I remember one particular time when my bus was already full to capacity and my conductor was having a hard time keeping late-comers from boarding. I jumped out of the cab and went to lend a hand. I pushed my way to the front of the queue and turned to face them. "I'm sorry, but you can see the bus is overloaded; you'll have to wait for the next bus in an hour's time."

A few backed off, but some of the drunker element were determined to have their way.

"There'sh plenny of room," one said. "Ger' out o'the way, man."

"That'sh right, Joe – you tell 'im."

Some of them pushed forward using foul language and threatening violence.

One chap, taller than the rest, pushed his ugly mug into my face and breathed alcohol fumes all over me. "I'm tellin' you. Get out o't'way," he shouted.

My blood was up by then and I seized hold of the front of his jacket and pushed him away with all the force I could muster. He staggered back about ten yards and then fell to the ground dragging a few of his cronies with him. A police sergeant was standing in the background, ready to step in if help was needed and the drunk caught sight of him.

"D'you shee that, offisher? That man – sh'd be appre – appre-nded. He ashault – ashaulted me."

"Did he, sir? I'm afraid I never saw him touch you. You'd better just stand there quietly until the next bus comes. Of course if you want to prefer charges, I can take you to the police station and you can wait there till the driver comes off duty. When will that be?" he asked me.

"Not for another two hours officer," I replied.

"Well, which is it to be, sir?"

The man muttered a few obscenities and backed away.

Now that the ringleader had been given his come-uppance, the rest of the trouble-makers faded away and we went on our way to Leeds. That was not an isolated incident. The racing fraternity were always more bother than they were worth, but it serves to illustrate the kind of co-operation we were able to expect from the police.

There were quite a few police whom I go to know socially. The Pontefract police had a cricket team and played matches at several of the surrounding towns and villages – Castleford, Featherstone, Sharlstone, South Hiendley, and so on. They had to lease a bus to transport the team when they were playing 'away' and they always asked for me because they knew I was a fair cricketer myself. Actually, modesty compels me to admit that I didn't have much finesse. My forte lay in having a strong batting arm and being able to hit a six now and then, so when the police team was a man short, because of an emergency, I was asked to fill in. I always enjoyed these occasions and later when S.Y.M. Co. formed their own team I was one of the first to join.

Two policemen whom I got to know very well were Sergeant O'Dwyer and P.C. Hardy, usually known as Bobby Hardy. They both lived in Featherstone and the colliery was part of their regular beat. At that time we lived in Colliery House as my father was now the caretaker of the colliery and my mother cooked meals for the members of the Coal Board and Colliery Managers when they held their monthly meetings in the large dining-room which was a part of Colliery House. I should say a word or two about my mother. She was a superb cook, not only of everyday things like roast beef and Yorkshire pudding, steak and kidney pie, home-made bread and teacakes, but things like pheasant and venison and other exotic foods. I'm not sure where she worked before she was married, but I'm sure it must have been with some upper-class family who could afford to keep a staff of servants. She never tired of cooking and made sure that my two sisters, Olive and Annie, learned to cook when they were quite young.

I remember one occasion when she was teaching Olive to make a stew and she said to her, "Always remember a stew boiled is a stew spoiled." And she made Olive repeat it several times.

The expression amused me so much it stuck in my mind and many years later when we were watching 'Upstairs Downstairs' I heard Mrs Bridges say exactly the same thing to the kitchen maid and for a split second I was back in our kitchen in Featherstone Colliery House, more than forty years earlier. I see my mother in the same situation as Mrs Bridges.

This may all seem irrelevant to the subject matter in hand, but believe me it is going somewhere. I mentioned that the Coal Board held their monthly meetings in our dining-room and they were invariably followed by a slap-up six or seven course dinner with appropriate wines. In those day the mines were owned by private companies comprised of affluent and often titled members, who were used to the very best in the way of food and drink. There was a large assortment of wines and beers in our cellar which was replenished automatically and we had the run of the wine cellar. We never abused this privilege; my father very rarely drank at all and my mother had only an occasional glass of stout. At Christmas time rules were relaxed somewhat. My mother made the traditional Christmas cake, rich, satisfying and soaked in brandy, and always made a dozen sometime in October to give them a chance to mature.

One Christmas Eve about 11:30 I was just coming home from the late shift when I met Sergeant O'Dwyer and Bobby Hardy on the colliery grounds. We exchanged pleasantries, remarked on the unseasonable weather – it was warm and wet – then on the spur of the moment I invited them in for a little Christmas cheer.

"We shouldn't really," the sergeant demurred. "We are on duty."

"A glass of port and slice of Christmas cake surely won't matter. After all it is Christmas Eve," I urged.

"Aye, go on then." The two men followed me into the kitchen where a fire was still burning even though the rest of the family was in bed.

The police took off their capes and put them over the backs of chairs to dry off.

I got out plates and glasses, went to the larder for a cake and to the cellar for two bottles of port, just to be on the safe side.

I poured generous helpings of port and cut several slices of cake.

"Help yourselves," I invited.

They didn't need a second invitation. The first slice of cake and glass of port went down smoothly.

"Your ma's a great cook, Harry," said O'Dwyer. "I never tasted cake like this."

"Have another slice," I urged and, of course, replenished our glasses.

"This had better be the last, Harry. We're meeting Inspector Clarke at the cross roads at 12:30 and he's a stickler for punctuality."

"Besides being a strict teetotaller," added Bobby Hardy gloomily.

"Aye he's a regular spoil-sport."

The sergeant seemed lost in thought for a few moments; then, "Give us another glass, lad."

So we all had another glass and another slice of cake and then a repeat. It seemed as if O'Dwyer was throwing caution to the winds and thumbing his nose at Inspector Clarke.

Hardy followed suit, after all if sarge could do it then so could he. The wine flowed more freely, the second bottle was broached, jokes were exchanged becoming broader as the level in the bottle went down. Laughs turned into sniggers and giggles; the second bottle was almost empty and the cake all done. Suddenly in a momentary lull the grandfather clock began to chime and then strike two.

"Bloody 'ell!" O'Dwyer jumped up knocking over his chair as he grabbed his cloak. "T' inspector will play the dickens." The shock seemed to sober him momentarily.

"Ne'er mind sarge," giggled Hardy, "e'll just say you're under the affluence of incohol and then you can shay I'm not sho think as you drunk I am."

O'Dwyer forgot his moment of sobriety and joined in the howls of laughter that followed this witticism.

I saw them off the premises and watched them out of sight, arms round each other and lurching from side to side. It was more than a week later before I heard of the outcome of our Christmas Eve festivities. We were at the Pontefract bus terminus waiting till time to set off for Leeds and I saw Bobby Hardy approaching. I jumped out of the cab and went to have a word with him.

"Happy New Year, Len," I said.

"Aye," he said gloomily.

"Got it in the neck for Christmas Eve?" I guessed.

"Aye, two weeks suspension, rotten bugger, after all it's only once a year."

"What happened to O'Dwyer?"

His face brightened and he began to laugh.

"You shudda been there, 'Arry. T' inspector were standing there looking at 'is watch, 'is face like a thundercloud when sarge suddenly pulled 'is cape over 'is 'ead, bent down, put 'is 'ands on t'ground and started prancing towards Clarke, growling like a bear. I didn't know w'ere to put meself. I wanted to laugh, but daren't. I stood to attention ꞥnd 'oped 'e wouldn't notice me. T' inspector seemed struck dumb for a minute, while sarge kept growling and pawing at 'im.''

" 'What the devil do you mean, coming on duty in such a state, you drunken sot?' said Clarke. 'Clear off before I fetch you one with my truncheon. And you'd better go too, Hardy. You seem to be a bit more sober than this fool. Tell them at the station to send replacements and I'll see you both in my office at 8 a.m. on Friday.' "

"Yes sir," I said and saluted and marched off dragging O'Dwyer by his cape.''

"What happened on Friday ?"

"We 'ad to report to Chief Constable and 'e didn't 'alf give us a dressing down. Said we were a disgrace to the force and if 'e 'ad 'is way we'd both be court-martialled." (The Chief Constable was an ex-army officer.)

"Anyway, after 'e cooled down a bit 'e gave me two weeks suspension, but 'e came down on sarge like a ton of bricks – demoted him to constable, gave 'im a month's suspension and fired 'im from 'is teaching job."

I should explain here that O'Dwyer was a teacher at the Police Training College in Wakefield which brought him a nice bit of extra pocket money.

"How did O'Dwyer take it?" I asked.

"Ooh 'e were as mad as 'ell – 'I'll get that bastard for this if it's the last thing I do. You mark my words,' 'e said.''

And he actually did – much later, during the war, but it was no concern of mine and not relevant to this story.

CHAPTER VIII

DRIVER-INSTRUCTOR

By about 1935 I was one of the senior drivers at S.Y.M. – not in age, but in experience and as the company grew, of course, they needed more drivers. Along with a few others I was asked to take on the job as driver-instructor; this usually meant working on our day off and we were only paid the regular rate, but there was quite a bit of prestige attached to the job and the extra money never came amiss. Quite a few of the conductors fancied being drivers. If they stayed with the company it was the only way they could better themselves and earn more money, so they were among the first to learn.

Willow Park was a large field on the outskirts of Ponte. It is now a housing estate, but then it was a sports field used mainly for football practice. There was a dirt and gravel track all the way round the field and this was where we gave our driving lessons. The conductors were eager to learn and by observing drivers at work had picked up a few of the rudiments of driving, so it wasn't long before they could drive. The most difficult part came later: learning how to handle a large vehicle, stop and start smoothly, stop at the bus-stop and not a bus-length ahead, and how to overtake in traffic, allowing for the length of the bus. I used to draw a line on the track and have the driver practise until he could pull up on the line. Then I would outline a large rectangle and tell them,

"This is a lorry ahead of you – moving a bit slower than you – pull out and pass him. Allow for his length, his speed, and the length of the bus, before you pull in."

That one took quite a bit of practice, but eventually most of them acquired sufficient skill to pass the Traffic Commissioner's Examination at Leeds. There were one or two however, who never made the grade: take Bert Higgins for example. He was a footballer playing mostly for his home team Castleford, but at one time he actually played for England against Australia. You couldn't wish to meet a nicer person, friendly, hail-fellow-well-met and ready to lend anybody a hand, but as a bus driver he was a complete washout. You may wonder why a famous footballer would want to become a bus driver, but this was during the depression and in the off-season he had to earn his living. He approached our traffic manager who was a friend of his and asked if he could be taught to drive a bus. So one after another the driver-instructors took him on a short run and each came back with the same response, "He'll never make a bus driver." And then it was my turn.

Bert could already drive a car, so all he had to do was learn how to handle a larger vehicle. We went out on a Thursday afternoon (early closing day) and before we set off I gave him the same warning I always gave, "Be aware of the width and length of the bus especially when turning corners, overtaking and parking." There were no passengers but we had to pick up some school children at Askern and take them home to Whitley Bridge and Knottingley. My conductor, Henry Claughton, was with us and of course I'd be driving when the kids were aboard.

The bus was already on the stand. Henry and I got inside and Bert got in the cab. He started the bus up – quite smoothly, accelerated and drove towards Ropergate where we had to make a right turn. The shop on the right-hand corner was sporting a large overhead canopy which reached beyond the edge of the kerb but we were on the left, so there was plenty of room to pass – I thought – and so apparently did Bert. We had barely reached the entrance to Ropergate when he turned the wheel to the right with careless abandon and swept down the awning, metal framework and all, and then proceeded merrily on his way, completely unaware of the mayhem he had created. Henry clutched my arm; he was as white as a sheet.

"For 'Eaven's sake, 'Arry, stop 'im. 'E's a ruddy lunatic."

"It's O.K.," I said hopefully. "There's nobody about." We were now approaching the Crescent Cinema where we had to make a left turn and fifty feet further on another left turn onto Southgate and from then on it was smooth sailing until we reached Knottingley. I held my breath and crossed my fingers as Bert swung the bus left and left again. He mounted the pavement at one point and came down with a bump that made our teeth rattle and then he was off like a horse making for its stable. I slid open the window to the driver's cab.

"Just go easy, Bert," I said. "You're already over the speed limit and..." as he turned his head round to answer me, "for God's sake keep your eyes on the road and one more thing – watch your distance from the kerb. You're driving too near."

I might as well have talked to myself. Minutes later, when we were about half a mile from Ferrybridge crossroads, we saw a farmer ahead of us with two horses. He was riding the one on the left and leading the other and going in our direction. Bert put his foot down and pulled out to overtake them and did so with a couple of inches to spare. If the farmer had been riding the other horse he would probably have lost his leg. The A.A. man on duty at the crossroads saw what happened and put out his hand, showing with finger and thumb how close we had been to the horses. Bert thought he was waving to him and waved back.

I thought Henry was going to faint.

"You've got to take over,'Arry – 'e's going to kill somebody."

"He'll be O.K." I tried to sound reassuring but it was a feeble attempt. "It's not far now and there's nobody about."

Famous last words. About two miles further on we saw a woman ahead of us pushing a pram and once more Bert misjudged his distance and practically grazed the edge of the kerb as he passed her.

I went to the driver's window and, as soon as the road was clear, said, "Pull over, Bert, I'll take it the rest of the way."

He stopped the bus and as I opened the door he tried to remonstrate.

"Get out," I said savagely. "Now!"

He got out.

"But Harry..."

"Watch me carefully," I snapped. "See how far I keep from the kerb and perhaps I'll let you try again on the way back."

Without further incidents we went on to Askern, picked up our busload of school children and dropped them off at Whitley Bridge and Knottingley. Henry had recovered from his fright and was his usual efficient self, shepherding our juvenile passengers into the bus, keeping their high spirits under control and seeing them off the bus and across the road safely when they reached home.

The bus was empty once more.

Bert came up to me.

"I watched you just like you said,Harry. I'm sure I'll manage better if you'll let me drive back to Ponte."

Henry gave me an imploring look, but I ignored him.

"O.K. I'll give you another chance. I think by now you should be able to gauge the width of the bus. Let's go."

He got into the cab and drove to Ponte with due care and attention. Henry and I began to relax. He made a right turn into Gillygate and even kept to the correct side of the road; next was a left turn into Horsefair, another right onto Cornmarket and we were home free. Henry and I were discussing our chances at the next cricket match when Fate in the shape of Bert stepped in once more.

There was an ear-splitting screech, as if a super-strong man was ripping a sheet of tin. I was sitting at the front of the bus on the driver's left and immediately saw what had happened. There was a lorry outside England's Ironmongers. The tail-gate was hanging down and at each side of the lorry was a metal peg used for fastening the gate when it was closed. Bert had driven so close to the lorry that the metal peg on the right had ripped right through the bus's panelling.

Again, sublimely unaware of what he had done, Bert drove the bus into the garage, jumped down and went to report to the manager. Henry and I, thankful to be all in one piece, made our way to the mess room. We were going back on regular service in about ten minutes and needed a good strong cup of tea to revive us. Barely had we sat down, when Ben Butler, the office clerk came in.

"Mr D. wants to see you right away, Harry."

"Tell him I'll see him when I get back. I'm due out in less than ten minutes and I'm not going without my tea for anybody."

Ben hesitated a few seconds, but he could see I meant it, so he went off to report to the boss.

When we got back from Leeds it was turned six o'clock and the office was closed. I put in my report when I came off duty and that was the end of Bert's attempts to be a bus driver. The manager was partly to blame for all the damage; he'd had several reports on his incompetence as a driver, but because Bert was a friend he let him keep trying. The insurance company paid for the damages and that was the last we heard about it.

I can't remember now how many people I taught to drive. Two

names in particular stick in my mind and that's because they became particular friends of mine: Bobby Burns was one. He was stout, dark-haired and had dark, twinkling eyes. He had a keen sense of humour and was always ready for a lark. Pop Moxon, was also dark and fond of a joke, but both of them took their work seriously and were very conscientious when learning to drive and both became good drivers. However, neither of them was mechanically inclined and they tended to be nervous if the bus they were driving became temperamental: backfiring or stalling on hills, etc. Eventually they both quit driving and became inspectors.

I came home one evening about 7:30. I'd been on a split shift since 5 a.m. and was looking forward to relaxing in an easy chair with the evening paper, but Mum was entertaining company, Mr and Mrs Laking, Percy and Edith. They were neighbours and good friends, so I didn't have to worry about entertaining them. We exchanged greetings, Mum poured me a cuppa, and I took a large slice of cherry cake and prepared to listen.

"Edith tells me they're getting a car," Mum said.

"Oh yes. What kind?" I asked.

"A Morris Oxford. Of course it's not new; it belongs to Edith's sister," Percy volunteered.

"I didn't know you could drive."

"I can't but ... "

"We were hoping you wouldn't mind giving him a few lessons," his wife broke in.

"Edith, you promised you wouldn't ... " he muttered.

"Oh Harry won't mind, will you? We'll pay you, of course."

"Nothing of the kind," Mother said. "You don't charge friends for a little thing like that."

I wished she'd leave me to make my own decisions. Percy was the chief wages clerk at the colliery and wasn't short of money and could easily have afforded to pay for lessons. I probably wouldn't have charged them anyway; I just wanted to decide for myself.

"When do you want to start?" I asked Percy.

"Whenever it suits you, Harry, if you're sure you don't mind."

"It'll be a change from teaching boneheads how to drive buses," I grinned. "How about Friday evening – about eight o'clock."

"Fine! I'll be waiting for you and thanks a lot," he said.

I brushed aside his thanks, thinking this would be a doddle. Will I never learn? The conversation then became general: about neighbours, work at the colliery and our respective families.

It was about ten to eight when I got to Percy's house on Friday evening; they only lived a couple of streets from us.

It was a nice car and in good condition and Percy was obviously very proud of it.

"Well, Percy," I said, "we'd better get started. Are you familiar with the way the car works? Do you know where everything is?"

"Not really." He looked a bit shamefaced. "I sat in the driver's seat, but I daren't touch anything."

"O.K. Well, I'll get in, show you how to start it up and drive around a bit and explain as we go along."

There was very little traffic in those days and I chose the quietest streets. After a few minutes I stopped, showed him how to start, accelerate and apply the brakes. Then we changed places and Percy began to drive. He was obviously very nervous, but he managed to drive along one street and then stop the car. It would be rather boring if I were to recount all the steps we went through. After about an hour I decided we'd had enough and made arrangements for the next lesson. I realized it would take longer than I thought for Percy to get over his nervousness and get used to the feel of the car.

At first I had him drive around a block of buildings so that he only had to keep turning left to arrive back at our starting point. Then as he got a bit braver we went further afield to Ackworth and East Hardwick, but as far as possible at times when there was little or no traffic. I had warned him about looking both ways when we came to an intersection, but one time when we were approaching East Hardwick crossroads, he turned left without checking and a car, approaching on our right, barely missed us. The driver sounded his horn angrily and shook his fist at us. This upset Percy so much that I had to drive us home. The next lesson, I decided, would be spent entirely on entering, crossing or turning at intersections.

Percy was way ahead of me. As soon as I arrived for the next lesson he said, "I'd better have some more practice at intersections hadn't I? It really shook me up last Tuesday."

I agreed and we set off towards Featherstone crossroads, but I wasn't prepared for what happened when we got there. About a bus length from the intersection Percy stopped the car and got out. He went up to the crossroads, looked both ways and then came back to the car and started it up. I had to laugh.

"That's no good, Percy," I said. "By the time you got back to the car there could be half a dozen vehicles approaching."

"Do you really think so? But there was nothing in sight either way."

"Never mind," I sighed, "drive on, but stop at the crossroads and look both ways – from the car."

He drove forward cautiously, came to a full stop, applied both brakes and spent a full minute watching the road. Finally he plucked up courage, released the handbrake and drove across. Once across, he pulled to one side and stopped the car.

"Was that O.K., Harry?"

"Yes, of course, but you don't have to put the handbrake on and you'll have to be a bit quicker. Once you get driving in traffic nobody's going to want to sit behind you while you behave as if you're driving a hearse."

Poor Percy, I hadn't realized quite how nervous he was behind the wheel.

Well, we soldiered on and after about six more lessons I decided I could't teach him anything more. The only thing he needed was confidence and I couldn't give him that.

He'd had the final lesson and made arrangements to take his driving test. We were going back to his house, which was on the right-hand side of the road. There was no one around and he pulled across the road to where Edith was already outside waiting for him. She was beaming all over her face.

"Everything alright then?"

We both got out of the car and went towards her answering her at the same time.

"Oh yes, I think he'll be O.K."

"It's fine, love. I really think I've mastered it."

We chatted for a few minutes and then Percy said, "Well, I'll just put the car in the garage, love. I won't be long."

"I've just put t'kettle on. Have you time for a cuppa, Harry?" Edith asked.

"I'd better not, thanks all the same. Mum will have my dinner ready."

I was just taking my leave of her when we heard an almighty crash. Edith went white as a ghost.

"It – it can't be Percy, can it?"

"I don't think so. It didn't sound much like a car crash." But we set off in the direction of the garage. There was a gravel road opposite the house with a right-hand bend in it about fifty feet from the main road and the garage was along this road. Behind the garage was a shed and beyond that a hen-house, chicken run, and various allotments.

I couldn't believe the evidence of my own eyes. The car had crashed through the back of the garage, knocked over the shed, setting free a couple of ponies who were galloping wildly among the vegetables, knocked over the hen-house and sent the chickens squawking and clucking and running in every direction; the car had come to rest in an open field beyond the allotments. We rushed over to Percy who was standing beside the car, completely dazed. Fortunately, he was unhurt, but the car was a write-off. Apparently, as he was able to tell us after having been revived with a cup of strong, sweet tea, he had put his foot on the accelerator instead of the brake when he entered the garage and then, as the car didn't stop, he panicked and pressed harder and harder on the accelerator, thus creating the afore-mentioned mayhem.

After that episode I was glad to get back to the simple job of teaching bus driving.

CHAPTER IX

THE SOCIAL CLUB

I don't know who first had the idea of a social club, but everybody was for it and wondered why we hadn't thought of it before. We nearly always had to work split shifts: maybe three hours on, one and a half hours off and then five or six hours on, and you didn't get paid for the time you were off. Many of us lived too far away to go home for such a short time. Of course none of us had a car, so all we could do was sit in the mess room and drink tea, read the paper, or walk about the town. A club room would be a godsend. A general meeting was held to set ground rules, decide on membership fees (I think it was half a crown) and choose what facilities we needed. Then three of us set out to find a suitable venue. It didn't take long – a hotel quite close to S.Y.M. Co. had a top floor which was vacant. There was just the one room which took up nearly the whole space and a wash-room. There was a billiard table, small tables and chairs for playing cards, a counter and water heater, which we could use for making tea and instant coffee, and a few easy chairs in front of a fireplace. It seemed ideal and the landlord was willing to let us have it for a nominal amount. He realized it would be bringing in quite a few potential customers for the public bar. We purchased supplies and a small cupboard for storing them and the club was all set.

After a while, being on split shift wasn't nearly such a drag as it was before. We could spend a pleasant couple of hours playing poker or billiards or sit in front of the fire chewing the fat with no fear of interruption from management. Of course we still used the mess room on S.Y.M. Co. premises for short breaks, but that belonged to the firm – the social club was the property of the workers.

One afternoon Albert and I had just finished a game of billiards and
went to join Sid Huddlestone and Jack Baker by the fire when Barge
Smith came into the room with a broad grin on his face. Don't ask me
why 'Barge' – I'd never heard him called anything else, but it seemed to
suit him. He was quite a bit overweight and very full of his own
importance, because he'd been to the local Grammar School and the
rest of us hadn't gone beyond Council School, but in spite of that he
hadn't absorbed much culture and was quite crude and ill-mannered.
For example, one time when he was still a conductor he was on with me
and the bus was full. Barge was edging his way up the aisle collecting
fares when he came to a woman standing between two seated passengers who were obviously her friends; one minute she would lean
over to the woman on her left and say something and then turn to the
one on the right. Every time she turned one way Barge tried to squeeze
by on the other side, but before he got by she again blocked the
gangway in front of him.

"Excuse me, madam," he said, then. "Can I get by, missus?" next
time and finally as she continued to thwart him, "Get out of the bloody
way, you old cow," he snarled so that all the bus could hear him.

You will gather why he wasn't very popular. As usual he plonked
himself down and broke into the conversation.

"You'll never believe what happened on the way out of Doncaster.
By gow, I wish I'd had a camera."

There was a moment's silence and then Albert said what was
expected of him.

"I'm sure you're going to tell us, Barge."

"It was Adam. As usual I was just ready to set off from Doncaster
depot, when he was taken short and had to go to the Gents. I said
couldn't he wait, but he said it was urgent. So I turned off the engine
and waited. I must 'ave waited for ten minutes and still no sign of him
so I blew the horn, once and then again, louder. He bust out of that
door, braces dangling, fly undone and," he paused, "believe it or not,
carrying his false teeth in his hand."

It *was* funny and we had to laugh. I should put in a word of
explanation about Adam Morrison. He was what in Yorkshire we
called only tenpence to the shilling and I know we should have been
more tolerant of him, but he had the uncanny knack of putting his foot
in it which wasn't the outcome of a shortage of brain power, more a
kind of indifference to anybody else's needs or feelings; he just

wouldn't be told. His father was a well-to-do business man and rumour had it that he had tried Adam in the business, starting from the bottom and, since he could do nothing with him, he paid E.P. Bullock to give him a job.

We were still laughing when Percy Atack came in and wanted to be let in on the joke. He laughed, of course, and then said, "He'll never make a conductor. How long has he been here now?"

"About two years, I think," Jack replied.

"Ay, about that," we agreed.

"Well, what do you think we did on Sat'day? The missus was going to Castleford to visit her mum. She had the baby on her knee and when Adam went to her for the fare he said, 'And what about the child? How old is it?' Well, she's only six months old and that made the wife mad. She knew kids travel free till they're five, but what made her really mad was him calling the kid 'it'. Madge always dresses her up in pink frilly dresses and satin bows. You'd have to be a moron not to know she's a girl."

"I agree, he'll never make conductor," I said, "and passengers have him weighed up. I know some of 'em get away without paying their fares. He goes to one for the fare and he'll say, 'I've already paid, you great lummox', and show him a ticket from last time he travelled, and Adam hasn't got the gumption to examine it."

"They'll have to pay when the inspector gets on," said Jack.

"Well, of course, but they often get away with it."

Percy started laughing.

"Last time he was on with me on the miner's shift," he said. "They played a right game with him. One of 'em had some washers tied on a string and he'd drop it on the floor and make a jingling noise when Adam wasn't looking and then say, 'Hey, lad, you've dropped some change.' Some of the others played up to him, pretended to look on the floor and say, 'Yes, look, it's under that seat', and Adam would get down on his hands and knees and look for it."

We all laughed, but Sid was a bit half-hearted about it. I looked at him.

"What's up, Sid?"

"Oh, nowt I reckon. I just feel a bit sorry for t'lad; he can't help being so gormless."

"It's not his being gormless that's the problem," Albert said. "It's just that he never has a good word to say about anybody and if you try to make a joke of it when he does something daft, he won't admit he's done anything wrong. It's always somebody else's fault."

There were a few murmurs of agreement and Sid looked a bit happier. Sid was a big man, in width as well as height and his heart was as big as his size. He was one of fifteen brothers and his father had a big farm in Whitley Bridge: a very prosperous one which supplied large quantities of vegetables to Covent Garden. All the brothers I knew were like Sid, big and well-made; I expect they were used to eating well. I know when Sid and I went on charters together, after we'd had a meal, he'd go into the bus for a sleep while I went for a walk and when I came back he'd be ready for another meal. We all made fun of his size, but he always took it in good part. One thing we all agreed on, he was immensely strong. I remember one time we were at Pontefract Statutes Fair. I got him to try his strength at the weight lifting machine. I managed about two hundred pounds but when Sid pulled the lever the gauge went up to over three hundred and fifty pounds.

"But I still think something could be done with Adam," he said. "He's obviously getting nowhere here. Maybe Dad could give him a job, picking peas or grubbing 'taters'. He couldn't go far wrong with that."

"He wouldn't do it, Sid," put in Jack. "It's beneath him being a farm labourer."

"I suppose you're right." Sid got to his feet. "Well it's time I were off." And it wasn't long before the rest of us had to make a move to go back to work.

Well, now we had a sports club and a social club and we wanted to expand our horizons; get to know families and friends of our co-workers.

"How about a dance?" someone suggested and the idea soon caught on. We elected a committee to make enquiries about a hall, a band, refreshments, etc. They didn't have far to look for a room. Pontefract Town Hall was the only place with really suitable premises. It was already being used by the local dramatic society and the Gilbert and Sullivan group, so most of the facilities were already in place. Soon we fixed on a date, had tickets printed and set about selling them. One thing we forgot about until nearly the last minute was transport after the dance. The last buses finished about 11:00 or 11:30 p.m. and the dance wouldn't be over until 2:00 a.m. and none of us had cars. Finally, somebody suggested approaching E.P. Bullock about using

S.Y.M. buses and surprise, surprise! He said we could use company buses free of charge, so long as we provided the drivers. That wasn't much of a problem; we took it in turn to do the driving. We just had to wear dust coats over our best clothes.

Soon we had two dances a year. They became very popular and lasted until the social club disbanded during the early part of the war. At that time there was quite a bit of money left in the kitty so we decided to use it to buy an X-ray machine for the local hospital. Some of us went to see it after it had been installed and the plaque on the side of it read:

Donated by E.P. Bullock
and the South Yorkshire Motor Co.

As I remember the money donated by the social club wasn't quite sufficient to pay for the machine and Bullock made up the difference, but not to have our contribution even acknowledged was galling to say the least.

I've reached the end of my account of happenings at the social club and I haven't yet mentioned two people who became lifelong friends and had quite a big influence on my life.

Cliff Harrison was the one I've known the longest. I first met him in the twenties when I was working as a mechanic and spare driver at Heald's Motors. One morning on my way home from work I happened to get on the bus Cliff was driving. It was early in the morning and the bus was empty. After a while I became aware of a very pleasant baritone voice singing softly. If I remember rightly it was 'Largo al Factotum'. I moved to the front seat beside the driver.

"That's one of my favourite arias," I said.

"You an opera fan then?" Cliff asked.

"Oh yes. I have been for years."

I didn't say any more then, the bus was filling up and you can't really talk and drive, but when we got to Featherstone Depot we had a chance for quite a lengthy conversation. Cliff lived in Featherstone too and was a member of the church choir. They also put on concerts with celebrity singers; on one occasion they even had Heddle Nash. We arranged that I should go to the next concert. I only saw him occasionally for the next few years as he was working for B. & S. Motor Company. Later on when I left Heald's and went to work for Mrs Winder, Cliff went there too and remained with the company when E.P. Bullock took over. Soon we got into the habit of going to musical concerts regularly, first at Featherstone then later at Sheffield City Hall which was noted for its first-class concerts. Celebrities from all over the world would appear there, tenors Joseph Schmidt, Beniamino Gigli, and pianist Anya Dorfmann, to name a few. Our friendship progressed and when his father died and his mother moved to Blackpool to live with her daughter and help her run the boarding house she and her husband owned, it seemed the obvious thing for Cliff to come and lodge with us.

By now there was a lot of disturbing news from the Continent: the Spanish Civil War, ominous signs from the dictatorships in Germany and Italy. But as always we in Britain felt protected by the Channel and turned a blind eye to what was going on, following the example of our politicians, and life went on pretty much as usual.

Some time in 1937 Cliff and I were scheduled to take a Sunday School party from Ackworth to Bridlington. There were three buses and one of the teachers accompanying them was Edith Middleton, well known to both of us as she was a regular passenger on S.Y. buses.

When we got to Bridlington and the children with parents and teachers had gone down to the sands, Edith said, "I've arranged for two friends of mine who are staying at Filey to meet me here. How would you like to make up the party?"

What did we have to lose? Edith was a nice girl and we were sure her friends would be O.K.

Well, they were more than O.K.; they were two sisters Mildred and Kay Holmes. Mildred was small and fair, Kay was dark and taller. We took to them at once, Cliff to Mildred and I to Kay. After that we dated them frequently and to make a long story short we were married: Cliff and Mildred in 1941 and Kay and I in 1942, so Cliff and I became brothers-in- law.

The other person who was instrumental in causing a major upheaval in our lives was Ted Sampson. I didn't get to know him until after the war so he really belongs at the end of Chapter X.

CHAPTER X

WARTIME EXPERIENCES

So much has been told by every branch of media of the early days of World War II – the lighting restrictions, food rationing, the trial air raids which scared us all to death and then the false sense of security engendered by the 'phoney war' – that much of what I have to say may seem redundant. But sometimes firsthand experiences of a few individuals can be more enlightening than the much wider coverage given by even top-notch reporters; and acting on that premise I will talk about how the war affected me and the other drivers at S.Y.M. Co.

The lighting restrictions were the hardest to cope with. Curfews were imposed from the very beginning. At sunset every householder had to make sure that all windows were obscured with black-out materials and police and air raid wardens ensured strict observance of this law. One tiny chink of light showing and in seconds (it seemed) there was loud rapping at the door and a voice shouting, "Put that light out". Street lamps were provided with cone-shaped covers so that only a small circle of light illuminated the road and the bulbs were blue. All vehicles abroad at night had to have the headlights hooded and the top half of the lights completely masked with black paper. We could rarely see more than ten feet ahead and there were no friendly lights from houses and shops to cheer us on our way. I don't know if the constant peering and straining our eyes to see in the black-out was harmful to our vision or not, but I do know that when I came off duty and went into the lighted house I felt as if I were looking through a thick fog. Carrots were supposed to improve your vision in the dark and some doctors would give you prescriptions for sight. I suspect they were mostly Vitamin C.

As if all the foregoing was not hard enough to contend with, the winters of 1940 and 1941 were the worst that had been experienced in over twenty years, according to meteorologists. In Northern England the snow was not measured in inches but in feet and snow-clearing crews were practically non-existent as most of the men had enlisted. We ploughed our way through the snow, making deep ruts and the few cars that were on the road tried to follow us taking advantage of the paths we had made. Overnight frost came and made those ruts as hard as cement so that if you had to make a turn or cross them in any way the bus got terrific jolts and the steering wheel was wrenched out of your hand as it spun this way and that with every obstacle encountered. It was impossible to drive more than three to five miles an hour. They were forced to stop the trams in Leeds because the tracks were solid with snow. This was not a matter of a few days' bad weather; it went on for weeks. There would be a few days of milder weather, then snow would melt a little and run into pools, the ruts would become softer. You would think that things were beginning to improve, when bang! down the temperature would drop and solidify all that soft slush, and then more snow. And now that new covering obscured all the ditches and banks of solid ice so we couldn't avoid them and the buses were flung up and down, and from side to side. When I got home into the light I would find my wrists swollen to nearly twice their usual thickness with struggling to hold the bus steady. In the country areas at crossroads and in especially windy corners, the snow was blown into drifts higher than a double-decker bus. A round trip from Leeds to Doncaster and back usually took three hours; now we were lucky if we could do it in six. In the end the conditions were so bad and so many essential workers, especially in munitions, were prevented from getting to work that the troops were called out and with the use of flame-throwers managed to clear the snow and ice from major highways. This happened many times in those two wartime winters.

Fog was another problem. In one way there was a slight benefit in that we were allowed to use full-beam headlights since they would not be visible to the bombers. Because of that we were aware of the lights of oncoming traffic but, as I've said before, lights don't help much in dense fog. The particles of moisture reflected the headlights back at us and though it seemed lighter we still couldn't see any better. I remember one time driving through Hunslet into Leeds and getting completely lost. It was one of the times when the snow had been cleared so that trams were running and I was on a tram route. I could hear their bells, I was conscious of trams passing me and of one ahead of me, but I had no idea where the turn-off to the bus station was. Eventually the tram I had been following at a snail's pace stopped and of course so did I. The driver came round to the cab and asked where I was heading. When I told him he laughed.

"You're in luck; it's right ahead of you. Just come round me and you'll be bang opposite the turn-off."

I thanked him heartily and we were on our way. I couldn't have found it without his help. With the black-out and the fog it was too dangerous for the conductors to walk ahead and I might have been driving around for hours.

By the end of the first winter I, along with a lot of other drivers, had had enough of black-out driving and on my day off I went to Leeds Recruiting Office and after filling in forms relating to my ability and suitability for the job I was after – driver-instructor in the R.A.F. – I was given a physical and accepted. The officer in charge said I would be notified in a few days' time when and where to report. As soon as I got back I went in to give my notice to the clerk in the office. He looked a bit taken aback.

"Just a minute, Harry." He went out and returned very shortly with the traffic manager, Mr. D.

"What's this I hear, Jordan?" he said.

"I've signed up; I'm going into the R.A.F."

"You're not going anywhere. You may not have heard yet, but the government has made bus driving a reserved occupation, and not before time. We've lost at least half a dozen drivers in the last month, and we're going to hang on to the ones that are left. You'll have to face the fact that you can't be spared, Jordan." And with that he walked out of the office.

It was galling, but essential services had to be maintained. Miners, farmers, munition workers, teachers, a quota of doctors and nurses all came under the category of reserved occupations. In a lot of cases women were able to replace men as munition workers, farmers (they were called Land Girls) and conductors on buses, but no women drivers then.

We got accustomed to it. You can get used to anything, given time and after you'd learned to cope with the black-out and food rationing, life didn't seem very different. This period was what became known as the 'phoney war' and we began to wonder what all the fuss was about. We had seen films and heard radio reports of the bombing, and all sorts of atrocities in Poland and been warned that this kind of thing was what we must expect. When nothing happened we began to feel complacent. The little man with the black moustache and his evil minions would never dare tackle the British Bulldog!

Spring of 1940! The invasion of France, Belgium and the Netherlands and the B.E.F.'s ignominious retreat from Dunkirk gave us a rude awakening and as wholesale bombing followed, Britain prepared herself for a long and bloody battle.

Now the buses could no longer be used for purely civilian purposes. Many were commandeered to help in transporting the forces on manoeuvres and in setting up army camps. Four buses and drivers were seconded from the S.Y.M. Co. and I was one of them. The seats were taken out of the buses and they were then filled with army supplies: tents, stoves, food stuffs, guns and ammunition. Our first camp was on a large estate outside Doncaster and as we didn't get there till quite late we had to get down to essentials: putting up tents, setting up cooking facilities and so on. Of course most of the work was done by the military, but the four of us had just come off a day's shift and by the time the bus was empty all we wanted to do was sleep. We lay on the floor in sleeping bags prepared for at least a ten hour kip. Alas, that was not to be! We can't have had more than four or five hours sleep when Reveille sounded and that's one alarm you don't sleep through! We hadn't undressed the night before. I'm not sure if we'd even brought pyjamas with us, but now with one accord we made our way to the door of the bus. There were urgent needs that had to be attended to.

Jack Riley was the first to reach the door and was no sooner on the bottom step with the rest crowding behind when he came to an abrupt stop.

"What's up Jack?" I called from behind the other two.

"It's not what's up," he said. "It's what's down. Look."

We all looked where he was pointing. That field was the home of a large number of very healthy cows and they had laid out a deep and very extensive welcoming carpet for us. Nowhere was there the smallest patch of green on which to step. With one accord we went to the emergency door at the back. The carpet there was even thicker. There was no way to get round this obstacle. Treading gingerly through the morass we made our way to the latrines and then to wooden troughs filled with water for our ablutions. At least when we got to the cook-house we were pleasantly surprised by the food. After the skimpy rations of civvy street, breakfast was a banquet: tea with sugar, bacon, as much as you could eat, at least two eggs and heavily buttered toast. I know a lot of the troops complained about army catering, but what if the bacon was half raw or burnt to a crisp and the eggs runny or cooked solid, after unsweetened tea and toast and margarine, it was nectar and ambrosia.

The rest of the day was spent in completing the setting up of the camp. We all had plenty to do and were well and truly exhausted by the end of the day. Now for a good night's rest! What a hope! About midnight we were practically shaken out of our beds by the crump! crump! crump! of falling bombs. There were no air raid shelters; the only protection was under the vehicles and we scrambled to get under the bus. We lay there in the dark for some time. The sound of the aircraft died away and after a while we returned to our beds. There were no more bombs that night and next day we learned that there had been little damage. As I said, it was an enormous field. The ground was soggy after much rain and most of the bombs – there were sixteen in all – had fallen harmlessly into the ground and, apart from a few inoffensive cows, there were no casualties.

Most of the time we were with the army was spent transferring army equipment from one camp to another, following behind military trucks when they went on manoeuvres, virtually filling in anywhere there was a shortage of transportation. As I remember we spent two or three weeks in this way and then went back to our regular jobs until we were needed again. It's not for me to question the whys and wherefores of these repeated manoeuvres and the setting up of carefully camouflaged army camps. I'm sure it has all been recorded by historians. What we did hear via the grapevine and subtle hints on the radio was that there were spies – fifth columnists they were called – working for the benefit of the Nazis and passing on information about military objectives for the bombers. There was quite a lot of support in England for the Fascist doctrine – by a group known as the Blackshirts prior to and during the early days of the war.

To return to more personal experiences of life in wartime England, the northern counties were more fortunate with regard to bombing. In fact many children were evacuated from London and southern England to our part of the world. The coastal areas were bombed frequently – Hull got a terrible basting I remember – and during those times the sirens would sound and we would often hear the familiar drone of enemy planes overhead.

When Cliff and Mildred, and Kay and I got married, houses were at a premium as so many were being destroyed by bombs and no new ones built, so we had a terrible time finding somewhere to live. Finally in the autumn of '42 we found a very large old house in Mayor's Walk in Pontefract. It had been occupied for many years by two elderly ladies who used only two of the twelve rooms, so the house was in a terrible state. The landlord offered to let us live there rent-free for six months if we would clean and decorate it. It had large bay windows front and back on both main floors; it was four stories high at the back and three in the front. On the bottom floor there was a large kitchen opening on to the garden, a scullery with a stone sink and a pump. On the same floor there was a large cellar used as a still room, a larder under the stone steps and a coal cellar. And everywhere you looked there were curtains of black cobwebs inhabited by spiders as big as chestnuts. Mildred and Kay were both terrified of spiders so Cliff and I had to wage war on these pests before they could begin to move in. I don't propose to give a room by room description of our heroic efforts to restore that house. The main rooms were beautifully proportioned, high ceilinged and really a joy to work on and we strove manfully until a certain night in late summer. We had painted the front room pale green and cream, the girls had made matching green curtains, the dining-room and main bedroom were finished and we were laying carpet on the main staircase. It was at night because, naturally, we had to work during the day. Suddenly the air raid siren sounded. Cliff and I were air raid wardens so we had to go on duty. The girls took refuge under the cellar steps; Mildred was about eight months pregnant at the time.

Once outside we went about our duties, expecting to hear the all-clear any moment, but one plane sounding much louder came nearer and nearer. Looking up we saw he was dropping flares to illuminate his objective – presumably the railway lines and storage sheds – and the next instant the whine of a dropping bomb and then a terrific explosion. We dropped to the ground in the shelter of a high wall and heard again the sound of a falling bomb, but this time no explosion. Our house was only a quarter of a mile from the railway and the sound of the explosion had come from that direction, so as soon as the all-clear sounded we wasted no time in getting home.

There are no words to describe our relief when we saw the houses, all the houses in the street still standing. As we approached even in the dim light we could see there had been some damage, but our main concern was with our wives. We went round to the back and into the kitchen. Being half basement it was the safest place to be. Mildred and Kay were O.K. and overjoyed at our safe return. We couldn't explore the damage that night. Some of the windows at the front were broken and with the black-out we couldn't risk showing any lights. Also there was no guarantee that the marauder wouldn't return and we were worried about the bomb that hadn't exploded, so we stayed up drinking tea and talking until daylight. Then we went to inspect the damage.

In some ways we were very fortunate. There was no structural damage to the house, but the interior was a shambles. Nearly all the panes in those large bay windows were shattered and glass was everywhere, inside and out. But what was worse, the massive chimneys can't have been swept for years and mountains of soot covered the floors and clung to freshly painted walls and the new curtains. We started with the kitchen and got it reasonably clean. The soot hadn't penetrated the cupboards or the larder so we were able to prepare breakfast and were just sitting down to the usual tea and toast when there was a loud knocking at the back door. I went to answer it and a military official stood there.

"I'm sorry, sir, but there is an unexploded bomb just at the bottom of your garden and we'll have to evacuate the whole street. It looks like a big one. Have you anywhere to go to?"

We looked at each other for a minute or two; we had no friends or relatives within easy distance of our jobs.

"I know," Mildred said. "Sue and George. They have plenty of room. I'm sure they'd be delighted to put us up."

Sue and George were the girls' aunt and uncle and very good friends to us all. They lived in Hightown, Castleford, only about five miles away.

"What about these broken windows?" I asked the officer. "Anybody could get in while we're away."

"Don't worry about that. We'll see they're boarded up. Just get your things together as fast as you can and clear out."

We had no alternative. Soon all our arrangements had been made and we were on our way. Sue and Grorge made us very comfortable, but in spite of that we couldn't wait to get home and get on with the cleaning up. Every day we expected to be given the all-clear, but it was not until the tenth day that I met the officer who was organizing the demolition squad. I was coming out of the S.Y. offices and he was at the Leeds bus-stand when I got there.

"You'll be pleased to hear that we've finally defused the bomb and removed it," he said without preamble. "It's on display in Butter Cross if you'd like to see it. It was a five hundred pound armour-piercing bomb. I wouldn't give tuppence for your chances if it had exploded. You can go home as soon as you like."

I thanked him heartily and later, when we went to look at the bomb, we were overwhelmed at the size of it. There was a collection box beside it for the demolition squad and we gladly gave a lot more than we could really afford.

That was the extent of our firsthand experiences of bomb attacks and, although it seemed devastating at the time, I realize it fades into insignificance beside the ravages caused by air raids in London, Coventry, Birmingham and countless other large cities.

The war years rolled by notable, as far as we were concerned, only for the monotonous food, black-out driving and the tedious sameness of day to day living. When the war was over I had completely got over my love affair with buses and couldn't wait to get away from them. In 1949 I bought a haulage business from the owner who was retiring. It's true I was still driving, but at least I was working for myself and I began to make money. And then, believe it or not, I injured my back through lifting heavy objects and had to spend seventeen weeks in a 'recumbent posture'. I had displaced three discs in the lower part of the spine. After that I had no option but to sell the business and go back to bus driving.

I can't explain my state of mind at that time; in nearly thirty years I seemed to have made no progress at all. I was desperate to try something else and here is where Ted Sampson comes into the picture. He had been a driver for West Riding buses but, as he and his wife, Iris, lived in Pontefract, he wanted a job nearer home, so he applied for a job with S.Y. Motors and as one of the senior drivers there I was given the job of taking him for a test drive. He was an experienced driver and I had no hesitation in recommending him for the job. After the test we went into the mess room for a cup of tea and while we were there he told me about his wartime experiences. He had been in the R.A.F. and was sent abroad to Canada – Calgary, Alberta to be precise. He couldn't speak too highly of Canada and the Canadian people. He talked about the magnificent scenery, the gorgeous weather and the modern and convenient houses.

"I'm going back there as soon as we can raise the fare," he said. "You ought to go too, Harry. There's loads of opportunities there. You've no idea..." He was off again.

He and Iris came to visit us and brought pictures and photographs to show us. We talked about it many times. In 1953 Iris and Ted were off to seek their fortunes in Canada and after much deliberation, Kay, our son Jeremy (Jay) and I followed them in 1954.

THE END